SEARCHING FOR
Sir Humphre
And Other Tales From The Thames

Text and Photographs by

Chris Morris

TANNER'S YARD PRESS

First published 2008 by Tanners Yard Press

Tanners Yard Press Church Road Longhope GL17 0LA
www.tannersyardpress.co.uk

Designed by Paul Manning
Printed and bound by Alden Press

British Library Cataloguing in Publication Data
A catalogue record for this book is available from the British Library.

ISBN: 978-0-9542096-8-1

*except as specified on page 145.

Contents

Preface

While I want this to be seen as another in my series of photographic books, I have included a longer narrative text, mixing modern commentary with an element of memoir. This is drawn from several summers I spent on the river as a very small boy, and from subsequent involvements with the Thames. The *Sir Humphrey* of the title refers to the family boat my father bought in 1947; memory is supplemented by snippets from my mother's diary, a holiday journal also giving a flavour of immediate postwar life. The inclusion of a small number of archive photographs amplifies the historic resonances.

My first task, after introducing *Sir Humphrey*, is to try to find her today. Following that, references to the old boat, and the diary of her voyages, will recur throughout the text. Rather than following the river from its headwaters to the sea, my journey begins at Bourne End (where *Sir Humphrey* was based) to travel towards the source; returning to Bourne End, I then head downstream (although this geographical framework suffers a few out-of-sequence leaps up and down the river to suit the subject matter).

It is often said that the Thames is two rivers: the pastoral stream defining the lush Home Counties, and the umbilical connecting London to the sea. While not denying its changing nature, I have attempted to see the river as a single entity. This book does not seek to be a comprehensive catalogue of every circumstance to do with the river, but rather a representative selection of interesting features. I hope that these coalesce to produce a portrait of the Thames, true to today while still redolent of the traditions and culture of England's greatest river.

Chris Morris
September 2008

Facing page: The Thames at Newbridge

Foreword

To grow up on a river is to belong to a timeless tapestry. *Searching for Sir Humphrey* provides a narrative that draws me back to the still morning mist, the canoe slicing the meniscus and a water rat scuttling away into the reeds.

As Chris Morris has noted in his preface, the Thames is in many ways a tale of two rivers: the choppy waters of the hard-banked industrial artery feeding the city of London, and the languid upper reaches, their agricultural base punctuated by market towns (and the city of Oxford). Alongside this commerce and leisure are the stories of serious play, creation and preservation, and a family's weekends and summers, living on the move with their ration cards in immediate postwar Britain.

This book is about a pilgrimage in search of a childhood, and a timeline of the Thames that recaptures moments that all who have had the opportunity will recognise, and others can dream of.

Mark Whitby was a winner of the Devizes to Westminster Canoe Race in 1968
and is a former president of the Institution of Civil Engineers.

Piers of Old Blackfriars Bridge, London

Canoeing at Hambleden Mill, 1970

SEARCHING FOR

Sir Humphrey

In 1947 my father went away for the weekend and came home with a boat. It went by the unlikely name of *Sir Humphrey*, and any thoughts of changing it were stifled by tales of bad luck – changing a boat's name seemed to be the equivalent of shooting an albatross. *Sir Humphrey* was no easy-going day tripper but a thirty-foot ex-naval auxiliary in need of serious love and attention, whose provenance was rumoured to include action in the Dunkirk evacuation.

I grew up not exactly on the river bank but in that broad swathe of the Home Counties known as the Thames Valley. We lived in Downley, a village high on the top of the Chiltern Hills; below, a small brook called the Wye flowed past our local town, High Wycombe (high in the Wye Valley), and the valley contained many watery references – Mill End, Wycombe Marsh, Loudwater, before arriving at Bourne End where the Wye met the Thames.

Our cottage was surrounded by common land, rough pasture where a few horses and goats occasionally grazed. The ground dropped steeply into the head of a dry chalk valley then rose back up towards the village centre. In 1947, when I was four and on my way to school with my six-year-old brother, I remember seeing it covered in snow; with lowered eyes, I walked down, then up, to the village bus stop, my school satchel a mountaineer's back pack as I imagined these virgin white slopes to be the foothills of the still unconquered Everest. When I arrived in the village, the waiting number 35 bus, bold red with 'THAMES VALLEY' underlined on its side in tall gold letters, put me firmly in my place.

Above: The 'skipper' near Bourne End, with crew, c.1948; Facing page: Sir Humphrey.

Despite our sense of geographical belonging to the Thames, it was a strange situation to find ourselves suddenly so committed to being river people. My father seemed to me a very steady man and not given to exuberance, though he undoubtedly enjoyed a maverick streak. Second son of a farmer, he had become an electrical engineer and in the 1930s travelled the country installing telephone exchanges. On a motorbike ride home to High Wycombe from Newcastle in 1933 he crashed, and was unconscious for a week: for the rest of his considerable life he was sustained by carefully balanced chemistry which, mostly, prevented epileptic-type seizures. Perhaps bolstered by the wartime government's 'Dig for Victory' campaign, his farming background gave him a compulsion to see productive growth from the land; our large garden seethed with activity and my father toiled for long hours after work with a primitive garden plough, growing vegetables on its arid chalky, flinty slope. His enterprise and engineering skills (which would prove vital in the restoration and running of *Sir Humphrey*) may have come from his mother's genes. Kate Parker was the toughest of farmer's wives (whenever she came to stay she ruled us as ruthlessly as a First World War general) but she was a daughter of commerce, her family being the well-known furniture makers Parker Knoll.

Above: Dunkirk plaque;
Right: The author rowing two
brothers and a cousin, c.1950.

Facing page, left: Ken Townsend
at Bourne End; Centre: Ossie
Stewart at Hart's Boatyard,
Kingston; far right: Daphne III.

So what could have made the 'skipper' (as my mother referred to him in her diaries – she was the 'mate' and we were 'the boys' or 'A', 'C' and 'S') want a boat? Could a clue be that both his brother-in-law and another work colleague had a cruiser and a launch on the Thames? It would seem out of character to be 'keeping up with the Jones'. Perhaps his austere and frugal instincts drove him to a bargain, for he bought *Sir Humphrey* in the direct aftermath of the great floods of 1947, when it must have been a buyer's market. My eldest cousin was with him when he went to clinch the deal in Kingston and recalls it being almost impossible to reach the boat for the amount of water still running downstream.

When the flood had subsided *Sir Humphrey* was brought upriver to what was to be its base for seven years, Townsend Brothers' boatyard at Bourne End, the nearest point on the Thames to us at High Wycombe. My father spent a lot of time on renovations to the mechanics and to the accommodation, and by the summer we were spending weekends on board. There was clearly more to do. My mother's diary notes in measured tones the breakdowns suffered in those early days: *'Sent to Marlow to find lubricating oil at 1 o'clock on Sunday'* and *'Lucky the boys spotted* Marsh Mist *so we got a tow home'* are two not untypical examples, the second referring to her brother's boat.

I am the middle of three brothers and in the spring of 1947 we were two, four and six years old – too young to say "Dad – how can we run a boat when there is petrol rationing and most people can't even run a car". I do recall him saying to my mother, "Don't worry – we'll save fuel by coasting in neutral down the hill to the river," and of course, aged four, not retorting, "But what about the extra going back up!" We led quite humble lives and how we ran a boat in such austere times I can't explain. The diaries frequently refer to the difficulties of catering for the family at a time when many foods were still rationed. Locating a supply of fresh milk was a near obsession, and our diet was largely canned food: mention of tinned sausages, tinned milk, powdered potato, all mix readily with poetic descriptions of the tranquil river, the sightings of kingfishers and the ubiquitous breakdowns.

Searching

Memories of seven childhood summers, and subsequent experiences, will colour my commentary on the Thames, but first I feel I should make a decent attempt to find *Sir Humphrey*. After more than half a century that may be an impossible task. Could I find a seventy-year-old thirty-foot cruiser, outstanding from more modern craft with real brass portholes? Few other boats could boast that distinction. But who would help?

I'm sitting at my desk 'googling' 'Sir Humphrey'. Might I find some trace? Up comes a lead: Sir Humphrey Gilbert, the founder of the first English colony in North America, lived at Limehouse, on the Thames just below the City of London. It could explain the name but doesn't help the search. I enter 'Thames Conservancy', the old licensing body for river boats: all I get is a reference to the Environment Agency; boat licenses on the Thames are now their responsibility. One of the features of modernising and 'rationalising' quangos is there is no need for the care or consideration of old records, which I find in this case only go back to the mid-1970s and include no mention of a *Sir Humphrey*. Could a subsequent owner have risked the wrath of the albatross with a name change?

I decide to try a more direct approach. Townsend Brothers' yard at Bourne End is today a marina, but I am referred to Ken Townsend, who never worked in the business but grew up on the waterfront (Ken's father was the fifth of seven brothers and only the first four ran the boatyard). From an old snapshot of *Sir Humphrey* I make up a 'lost cat'-type poster and arrange to meet Ken. On the old wharf at Bourne End he tells me a potted Townsend history and shows me his collection of postcards. Many are from the 1950s, but regrettably none of the boats match. My 'lost boat' poster disappointingly fails to provoke Ken to a boyhood memory, but amazingly we find a connection: needing an older crew for a trip to London in 1950, the skipper recruited my eldest cousin Roger and his school friend – who turned out to be Ken. Both these 1950 seventeen-year-olds remember the trip down past Tower Bridge as far as Limehouse Reach after which an abrupt U-turn saw them heading for home. My cousin has a strong memory of the struggle to get back upriver; the skipper, more used to the placid waters of the upper river, neglected to consider the streaming ebb tide and poor old *Sir Humphrey* only just had the power to avoid being swept backwards downstream.

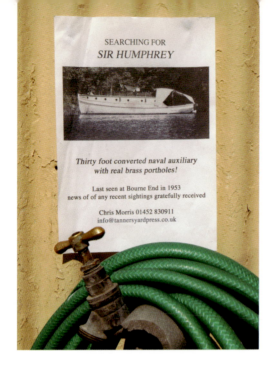

I have another hands-on attempt to make. I find that there is a boatyard at Surbiton, named Hart's, with claims to be the oldest on that part of the river, which specialises in restoration. I know that *Sir Humphrey* was bought in Kingston; it could be that this was the yard, and what could only be said to be a hunch has acquired a bit of credibility. Following my visit to Bourne End I know that there was a family connection between Townsend's and Hart's. The skipper quite possibly asked advice about a 'restoration' buy at Bourne End, his local boatyard. What could be more natural than keeping it in the family by directing him downriver to a yard run by their own relations?

Ossie Stewart, who took over Hart's in 1976, is really helpful on the phone and, amazingly, says that their ledgers go back to 1890! In due course I visit him, armed with my 'lost boat' poster. Ossie runs a business called Stewart Marine, mainly still restoring traditional Thames craft and also fitting out new residential long boats; Hart's has been subsumed into a very modern pub and restaurant business nextdoor. In his riverside office we look at the ledger and – sad to say – it does not go back as far as we hoped; its first entry is 1949, tantalisingly just two years away from my hoped-for 1947.

Ossie shows me his restored slipper stern launch, takes me into the adjacent Thames Yacht Club where he keeps his 'A rater' racing dinghy, both Thames classics, and offers me advice: he agrees with a colleague who is absolutely sure that a boat identical to *Sir Humphrey* is moored at Platts Eyot. I make this small island, upstream at Hampton, my next port of call. Under dark overhanging trees I walk the perimeter of the island (see page 53) buzzed by mosquitoes and braving nesting swans; *Daphne III* is the nearest match I can find and I feel a very long way from realising my quest.

After this dashing of my hopes I am beginning to see boats that are similar, though definitely not identical, in a different light. I half shut my eyes, imagine a cabin superstructure added, wonder how much the hull itself can be altered and seem to be in a dream world. Looking through old photos from West India Dock I notice in the distance a boat similar to *Sir Humphrey*; then realise that the stern is too long. Can boats be extended like stretch limos? I spend half an hour with Photoshop truncating this boat in my picture, in my dream restoring it. I write *Sir Humphrey* on the prow. I wake up and suppose I'll have to give up.

Top: The 'lost boat' poster; Below: Matilda II;
Bottom: Lazy Days; *Facing page:* West India Dock, 1980.

But two more near misses revive my interest in the search. Passing through Mapledurham lock I admire *Lazy Days*, strikingly similar to *Sir Humphrey* but slightly smaller. Proudly displayed on her cockpit side panel is a 'Dunkirk Little Boats' plaque, something our skipper often speculated on. Finally a sighting which lifts my spirits and makes all the others seem complete misfits. *Matilda II* is on a boatyard mooring on Sunbury Lock Ait; this is possibly the island Ossie Stewart had meant when he suggested Platts for it needs no imagination to see a *Sir Humphrey* clone. Through the boatyard I'm able to contact her owners who tell me details that match completely. It takes a measured scrutiny of her portholes to tell me that, unless they have been realigned, *Matilda II* is not *Sir Humphrey*. But there is another twist to the story. The owners tell me that in November 1995 Guy Nelmes, the secretary of Dunkirk Little Boats Association, (*Matilda II* has a Dunkirk plate) passed her on the river and said he knew of a twin.

This proves to be another false trail. Guy Nelmes remembers a conversation in 1995 but doesn't recall a twin! He is passionate about all things that relate to Dunkirk boats but at the time my text is off to the printers he has found nothing new to tell me.

Did I expect to find *Sir Humphrey*? Probably not, but its memory will colour the river journeys ahead.

Taming the Thames

From earliest times there would have been three groups of Thames users with conflicting interests in the maintenance of the river flow. First would have been fishermen, who learnt to put in weirs with traps for eels and other fish. The weirs would have suited the millers who used the river power for grinding corn, and later for many other uses, as they would value the increased 'head' of water; leats would be taken off the higher level upstream of the weir to power their water wheels. The group seriously disadvantaged by the barriers across the flow were the boatmen, for the Thames, like the Severn, was a great inland highway for trade. The vested interests of the fishers and millers gradually gave way to the needs of the transport lobby. Initially 'flash locks' were installed, essentially a removable section of weir. After the initial rush when the lock was opened, a boat would be physically hauled up against the stream; coming down was obviously easier. Laborious and inefficient, this system suited no one, though the weir owner gained revenue from it.

By the early seventeenth century the concept of a 'pound lock' was being put into practice, the first ones being at Iffley and Sandford. Most of today's locks weren't built until the late eighteenth century, when the canals formed a network of inland waterways able to service the surge in demand for transport generated by the Industrial Revolution.

By using a double pair of lock gates fitted with controllable underwater sluices, it was possible to match the level of the water between the gates to the level of the river above or below the weir. A boat heading upriver enters the open lower gates, which are then closed, and the sluices shut. Then the sluices of the upper gate are opened until the level in the lock reaches that on the river upstream. The top gates can then open. Heading downstream the process works in reverse.

The pound lock suited all parties, for there was no loss of head of water, the weirs still worked in parallel and transport was inestimably speeded and eased. Over the years the mechanics have become more sophisticated, so today most Thames locks use hydraulic power and are controlled by push-button electronics. Beyond Oxford the traditional manual systems are still in use; the gates extend into long wooden beams which are pushed to open them and the sluices are wound up and down by spoked wheels driving rack and pinions. Most weirs are also now under more modern control, making them easier to use and maintain and therefore safer. However, some sections of a few weirs still use 'rymer and paddle', an ancient and beautifully simple concept (but

heavily manual and slow in emergencies). The 'rymers' are a set of posts which drop into slots on the floor of the weir; the 'paddles' fill up the spaces between, up to three deep to block the full height of the drop. The whole mechanism is watertight because of the force of water pressure.

Keith Webb has been a lock keeper for nearly forty years, employed in turn by Thames Conservancy, Thames Water Authority, National Rivers Authority and today the Environment Agency. Far from welcoming the ease of elecronic control, he actually sought a transfer upstream to Grafton to be able to use the old manual systems. I asked him if strength was the big issue and he said: "No – it's technique. The only problem is if someone 'helps' me by closing the sluice before I have shut or opened the gate; the extra water that has to be pushed makes a surprising difference."

Above: Flash weir capstan, Hurley;
Left: Weir 'paddles', Mapledurham.
Facing page, top: Keith Webb, Grafton Lock;
Below: Lock keeper's cap badge from
Thames Conservancy.

15

Thameshead

A433

Kemble

A429

South Cerney

R. Churn

Castle Eaton

A419

A417

Fairford

A417

Lechlade

Kelmscot

Boveney

Buscot

A361

Faringdon

A417

A420

Grafton

A4095

Radcot

A4095

Rushey

Shifford

Duxford

A4095

A415

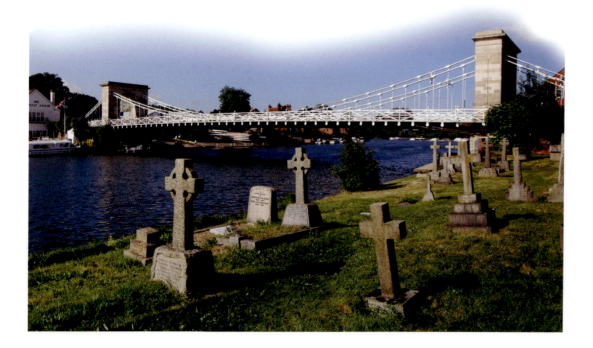

Above: Rowing trophies, Goring and Streatley; Left: Marlow Bridge; Facing page, top: Moorhen's nest, Hurley; Right: Thames Conservancy plaque, Day's Lock.

Note: Map placenames in blue indicate river locks.

Voyaging Upstream

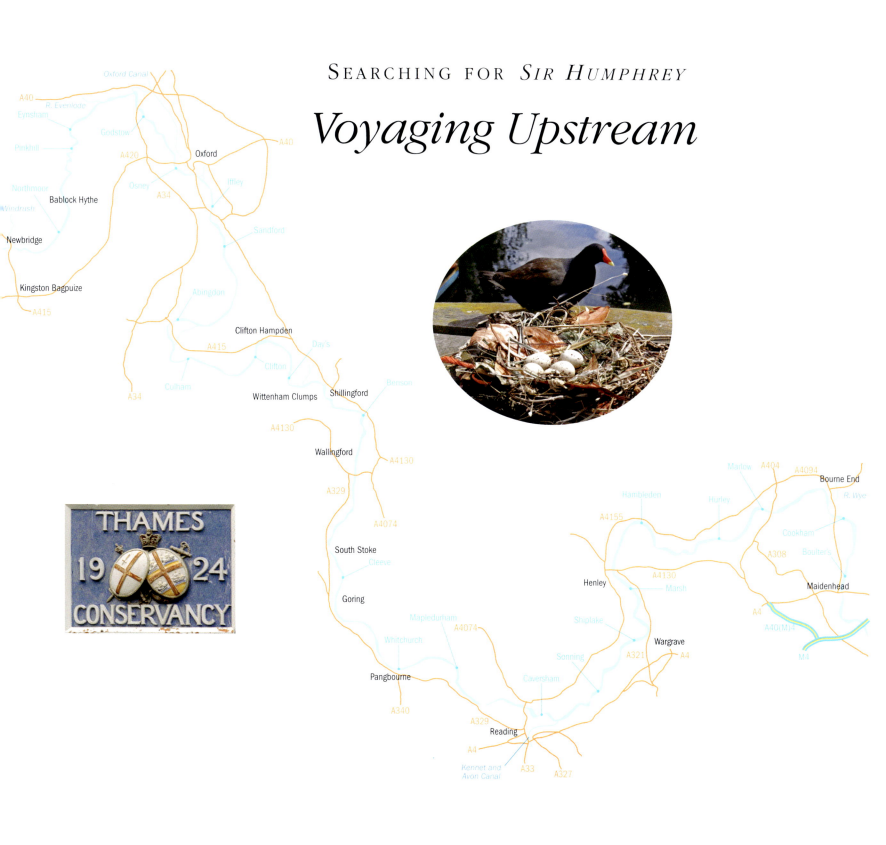

Fishing as a boy

It might be thought that at two, four and six years old we, 'the boys', were too young to be on a boat at all. The deck on *Sir Humphrey* had railings all around the edge and along the centre a long clothes line was strung from end to end; while on the move we were harnessed to this line with clips, like dogs on a lead, for some sort of mobility coupled with safety. The deal was that when we could swim we earned our freedom.

Our first trips on *Sir Humphrey* didn't take us far upstream. Towards Marlow, on the Berkshire side under Winter Hill, big houses with immaculate riverside lawns filled the banks; the Buckinghamshire bank had the towpath and pasture land. On this bank, a mile from Bourne End, the skipper's cousin's family had the use of a summer house where we became frequent waterborne visitors. Tied up next to a small river beach we practised our swimming, a priority, and also learnt to ride bikes on the towpath, to row in the dinghy and spent happy hours 'fishing' (hazel sticks, string and a bent pin). Learning to swim and to row had a bonus: as well as freedom from the dog lead, we were then allowed out alone in our little dinghy.

We spent day after day fishing – still with cotton and a bent pin with a cane for a rod. We caught nothing. My elder brother was a stoic, but it wasn't long before I was unhappy about the lack of success. From the diaries I can now read: 'C – "I wonder why we don't catch any fish?" A – "I expect it's that we aren't patient enough."' A couple of years later, with much parental reservation, I sought out a cheap ex-army fishing kit and by the time I was seven was a serious fisherman, rowing away in the dinghy, often at the crack of dawn, to favourite spots in reedy backwaters.

For my eighth birthday I was given a real fishing rod and tackle. The mate wasn't very pleased with the escalation of what had seemed a harmless hobby: '*the revolting creatures have started fishing with live bait – small minnows squirming on the hook – hoping to catch a pike.*' She wasn't too pleased either with our insistence that the hobby couldn't be seen as mindless cruelty if we sent the fish home to feed the cat; we played our part catching them, the skipper would take them home on his bike – the mate's contribution would be to gut and cook them. Unfortunately '*amongst the now cooked perch, gudgeon and roach were some 'pope' which C only then heard from a 'real' fisherman were poisonous.*'

At fifteen I wanted to recapture what I remembered to be the charm of fishing. I dug tasty bright red worms from our garden compost heap, found my old rod and tackle in the loft and caught a Thames Valley number 28 bus to the Thames. My mother had a friend who lived in a riverside bungalow half a mile downstream from Marlow, by the big bend where the lock cut joins in below the weir, and I'd arranged to borrow her skiff. I rowed downstream into dark water, reflecting Quarry Woods above, and in the quiet backwater tied up by the reeds to wait for old

times to kick in; but the magic was missing. Close by was Wooton's Boatyard, a treasure trove of restored Thames craft. Slipper stern launches were moored on the quay, and a pretty miniature steamer that I remembered admiring from *Sir Humphrey* days was still bobbing on its buoy; I found myself more interested in these than in the possibility of knocking two miserable perch on the back of the head to take home for cat food, went home empty-handed and disgruntled and vowed never to fish again.

Above: 'Big houses with immaculate lawns';
Facing page: Three boys fishing, c.1950.

Fishing at Marlow

Half a century later I have been persuaded to change my mind about fishing. Just above Marlow lock, adjacent to the weir and the beautiful suspension bridge, is the Compleat Angler hotel. Many guests ask about the 'incorrect' spelling, unaware of the reference to the title of the famous treatise on angling by Izaak Walton. This was his 'local' where he took his refreshment after fishing in the weir pool, and possibly wrote his book, first published in 1653 and with many subsequent editions.

At the hotel I am introduced to Roger Barnes, a professional fisherman who I believe may be the Izaak Walton of our times, for he has just written his own book. When I meet him I find that in fact his book is more social history than fishing manual. In the late nineteenth century a law was passed banning the netting of fish in the Thames; this enabled rod and

line angling to become a suitable 'gentlemen's pursuit' for the beneficiaries of the new industrial wealth. The railways, and ice, enabled the gap in working families menus to be filled with sea fish and, after the initial shock and hardship, the men who had earned their living supplying fish became professional 'fishing guides' (just like Roger himself today).

Like Izaak Walton, Roger too fishes below the weir and, he assures me, he'll catch a pike to show me. The hotel manager and the chef were enthusiastic about my idea that it could go on the restaurant menu, but we didn't allow for the concerns of the modern fisherman. Roger can't agree to catch a fish and kill it to eat – he and his colleagues feel that fishing today is more about conservation than cooking and so it would have to go back into the river.

On the morning when I go out in the boat to fish with Roger, he is with Californian software executive Steve Wozniac, extending his business visit for a few days' recreation. Actually Steve takes his fishing as seriously as his business. Back home he has a spreadsheet (he offers to call it up on his mobile) recording all seven hundred species he has caught, and many he still hopes to catch. Roger and Steve joke about the possibility of catching a 'pope', surprisingly one on Steve's wanted list, so I tell him of my childhood cat food story.

Apparently it is a myth that the pope is poisonous – its reputation as a bad fish is because a scratch from its spiny dorsal fin can give an irritating rash.

Luckily Steve had fished a pike out of the pool within thirty seconds of arriving, while Roger was setting up the boat, as for the next two hours we didn't catch a pope or a pike or even bleak for bait. Just as well the restaurant wasn't waiting on us!

Above: Pike stained glass at the Compleat Angler hotel;
Right: Fishing below Marlow weir: Facing page: Roger Barnes
and Steve Wozniac with a pike.

Wooton's Boatyard

Determined to find that pretty steam launch I remembered so well, unannounced I descend the winding lane down Winter Hill and see Wooton's appearing below me through the trees. At least the yard is still there: indeed, I discover it is thriving and about to celebrate its hundredth birthday. Traditional skills flourish and blend seamlessly with modern materials – for instance, the planks of a skiff being renovated consist of the traditional cotton caulking sealed not with putty but a modern mastic.

Guy Wooton and his son Lee, fourth and fifth generations of the firm, pose for me in front of a new shed built specially for the restoration of a fast sea launch, built in the USA in 1935 for the President of Paramount Studios, who used it to commute to work in Boston. Wooton's is the last stage in its journey from Massachusetts: after crossing the Atlantic to Liverpool as deck cargo, it went by road to the Thames above Marlow, from where it was floated on pontoons down to the yard. Its Bourne End owner will finally sail it down river and across to the French Mediterranean.

I ask about the pretty steamer of my memories, find she was called *Pierrette*, but is long gone. A sense of mystery seems to hang over her whereabouts. A Shiplake museum is mentioned, but no references are available. We talk of classic Thames boats and I get a very helpful lead to another iconic steamer, *Alaska*, which I find later in the day.

Above: Lloyd Loom chairs in a slipper stern launch;
Facing page: Lee and Guy Wooton, of Wooton's Boatyard.

Pierrette

Back home, I google 'Shiplake boat museum' but only get the Henley River and Rowing Museum – which sounds very interesting but is clearly not what I am looking for. I speak to Peter Green, owner of *Alaska*, and also mention *Pierrette*: He suggests I contact Colin Henwood who has a boatyard at Hambleden and helped the owner with restoration work. I find that *Pierrette* is part of the Rose Collection, but this is a very private museum – no contacts can be given out but my interest can be reported. I must have made a reasonable impression, for the following day I get a phone call from William Rose and forty-five minutes later he has agreed that I can see this fabled boat.

The Rose Collection is a treasure trove, with artefacts running from 1840 to 1940 and boats from 1890. Everything is absolutely immaculate – as Bill Rose says, he is only interested in the very best. *Pierrette* is a forty-foot steamer, steel-hulled, built by a man named Desvignes in Chertsey in 1894. Sadly the difficult logistics of getting her into the river mean that happens only once in ten years, so I had to view her in the boathouse: even there she is dazzlingly beautiful, but it's hard to take a photograph that does her justice! Bill tells me a little of his background: a farmer, then in business in the city, finally spending all his time, with his wife Penny, on his beloved collection. In the late sixties there was little interest in restoration; he felt that the tradition and craft were important but risked being lost. He had already started buying up

classic river boats when he decided to search for *Pierrette*, which he remembered, just like I had, at Wooton's yard. Long sold on, his only information was that she was somewhere in Norfolk, but that did not deter him. "I went to stay in a Norwich B and B and scoured the rivers and Broads until I found her, then made an offer her owner could not refuse".

It was clear that I was very privileged to be shown Bill's collection and I wondered why I had been so lucky to get the invite. Possibly it was the similarity of our tangential experience with *Pierrette*, noticing her at Wooton's, the gestation of memory which culminated with Bill buying her and me finding her, that appealed to him. Taking tea on the balcony overlooking the river we came up with a remarkable coincidence and another common strand of history: it turns out that his Buckinghamshire farm was only a couple of miles from that of my grandfather (then my uncle and my cousin).

Facing page: The 'Bill Rose Collection';
Above: Bill Rose with Pierrette.

Alaska

Meanwhile *Alaska* is going to be out on the river for a series of bank holiday trips. Owner Peter Green had invited me to meet him at his moorings upstream of Temple Lock but the weather was literally a washout ('Red Board' warnings were out, meaning no craft on the river). Two weeks later we had a new rendezvous for me to see his beautiful boat, at the Compleat Angler at Marlow; a party of tourists, lunching there, were to be treated to a trip to Cliveden.

The photograph opposite is taken approaching Bourne End – appropriately, as that is where, in 1883, she was built (double diagonal teak planks on an oak frame) by J.S. Horsham, as a hire boat for local pleasure trips. After three years Salter's Steamers bought her and in 1887 she was used to inaugurate their Oxford to Kingston passenger service. From 1939 she went through a variety of owners and jobs and ended up with her engine removed, being punted up river to Oxford. There, ignominiously, she was used as a base for a boy scout troop who, the story goes, chopped up her superstructure to sell as firewood to raise money for a new hut! *Alaska* was discovered in 1974 at Medley Boat Station sitting on the bottom, decked with plywood and used as a pontoon. Finally rescued, she was fitted with an outboard motor and taken down to Peter Freebody's yard at Hurley (see page 60) where she spent the next twelve years; her complete restoration included, amazingly, being refitted with her original engine. As we have seen today, age notwithstanding, she is kept busy on private charter and local pleasure trips.

Above: Alaska *in full steam;*
Facing page: Peter Green, skipper of Alaska.

Peter Freebody

One of the best known of the traditional boatyards on the middle Thames is Freebody's, tucked away in a backwater at Hurley. On the day I visit, classic slipper stern launches, originally developed by Andrews of Maidenhead, are much in evidence, their unique varnished sterns glistening in the sun. When I was a boy, these boats were the common currency of boat hire – available by the hour to all comers. Today they are prized collectors' items, but still being built here in the traditional manner.

Richard and Melanie work with their father Peter, whose pose for me on the jetty seems reminiscent of Old Father Thames (upriver on St John's Lock). I ask Peter how many generations of his family have been in this business: he replies that he doesn't know, but they have been boat- building since the eleventh century!

Top: Peter, Richard and Melanie Freebody;
Right: Statue of Old Father Thames at St John's Lock;
Facing page: Slipper stern launches, Freebody's.

Top: Henley Regatta course, on a practice day;
Above: Flags flying, Henley Market

Henley – regatta town

For some, Henley is best known for Brakspear's Brewery, for others Hobbs' Boatyard. Of course for most people the town is synonymous with the Royal Regatta. As Brakspear's has been bought out (and it's Henley premises closed down) and as Tony Hobbs no longer builds boats (though still runs a busy hire and river cruise business), the regatta seems a clear winner.

Henley stands for more than four days of racing boats up the river: along with Wimbledon and Ascot, it is in the premier league of the Home Counties social scene, with rigid protocol on members-only enclosures and strict dress code. To reflect something of what Henley stands for, I had hoped to take a stylised shot of the Umpires and Stewards showing off the trophies, perhaps before the hurly burly of race days. That was to be utterly impossible: the silverware is locked in the trophy cupboard and the cupboard is in the 'Steward's Enclosure' which photographers are not allowed into. I was to apply for press accreditation – maybe I could go out on an umpire boat, but no – my application was refused.

So I decide to visit Henley the week before their big jamboree; the town is busy with anticipation, all the tents are up and crews are practising on the river up the famous course laid out from Temple Island. Cabin cruisers thread their way heavily around the fragile eights and sculls, just as I remember *Sir Humphrey* doing (on another occasion the diary reads *barged our way through Maidenhead regatta*). In fact, then and now, the right of navigation remains paramount, with a channel staying open to non-regatta traffic. The skipper may have been a maverick but could also be respectful: in another entry the mate complains *told to take down the washing from the line as we were going to Wallingford Regatta: I had thought it would do as flags!*

The town's riverside extends upstream above the bridge, past Hobbs' boat hire quay and on to the River and Rowing Museum; inside the striking modern building (with car park and cafe!) the museum offers a great sense of history with many classic boats and artefacts on display. Opposite, on the Wargrave bank, traditional boatbuilding continues as Hobbs' old yard is still in use by their long associates, the Brownjohns.

Top: View of Henley Bridge from the Angel Inn; Above: Alan and Paul Brownjohn, boatbuilders.

Above: Henley sartorial style.

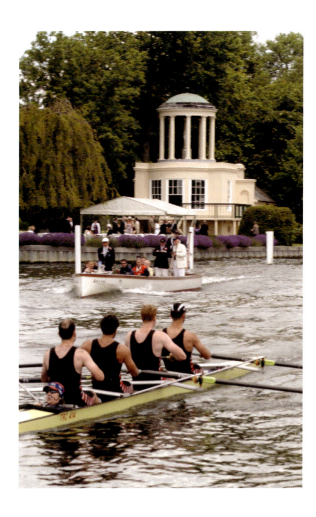

Henley – race day

A week later and I feel I should visit Henley during the competition. I have a cunning plan to avoid the traffic, driving on lanes down the Chiltern valleys I know from childhood to arrive at Hambleden's Mill End. From there it is a walk over the long weir to reach the towpath a quarter of a mile from the Temple Island regatta start line.

I'm still a long way from the high point of the social scene but even so most people thronging the public and private bars and enclosures look as though they are on their way to a wedding. Except those in blazers who look as if they are at Henley. On the river the races struggle to compete for attention with the fashion; jugs of Pimms apart, the whole scene is reminiscent of a rather select primary school sports day where there is continuous action on the track but no-one is sure which race it is.

Is the dress protocol under attack in the twenty-first century? Clearly Simon Read, the builder of the new umpire boat *Heracles*, was not fussed to dress up for his delivery photo. And the shopkeeper whose window shows a t-shirt and baseball cap is offering a very radical alternative to tradition.

Top left: Racing, at the Temple Island start; Left: On board Heracles, *the new umpires' launch, left to right: Mike Sweeney (Regatta chairman), Simon Read (boatbuilder) and Colin Hinton (driver); Right: Local shopwindow display.*

HERAKLES

*Above: Fishing sign,
Shiplake; Below:
Memorial to Peter Gough,
lock keeper; Bottom: Lock
keepers Andy Feak (left)
and Daniel Popper (right).*

Shiplake

We had several favourite mooring locations for our stays on *Sir Humphrey*, often for weeks at a time while the skipper commuted to work by bike, or only came visiting at weekends. Just upstream from Henley, Shiplake was our last discovered and best remembered; I suppose by ten years old, memories linger longer.

Our chosen spot was in the lock cut opposite the weir; we swam in the little bay, just where a local couple sit enjoying a glass of wine on a summer evening in 2008. Despite the Binfield Heath anglers (who I think were simply amused at our puny efforts) fishing was still the most important thing in my life (*C given a keep net for his tenth birthday – went on a bus to Henley to buy maggots*). Apart from this obsession our social life revolved around the proximity of the lock where the lock-keeper, Mr East, occasionally allowed us to help with the sluices. The skipper spent a lot of time talking to him about river matters, including the 1947 floods which in 1950 were a very recent and vivid memory. As reported to the mate he told of the inconvenience: *he and his assistant couldn't get to the toilet for ten days* and of the danger: *how the only way to keep the weir clean was by dinghy and one had to be brought to him from Reading.*

I'm visiting Shiplake for the first time in fifty-five years. Is there any chance today's lock keepers could remember Mr East? Andy Feak and Daniel Popper are a relief team who work on a rota – two days every week at Shiplake – and even though Andy has worked as a lock keeper for thirty years (and has no plans to stop) the answer is no. They point me to a memorial seat in the garden, from which I deduce that Mr East left Shiplake in 1954, the year after our last stay. The bench is dedicated to lock keeper Peter Gough who in 1982, keeping the weir in order, fell in and drowned. On a sunny day in June, with the lonely cold winter months seeming very distant, Andy and Daniel both agree what a lovely life it is; for them the variety their rota gives is a bonus while still allowing an attachment to Shiplake.

Above: Evening drinks at the spot where Sir Humphrey *moored.*

While the skipper was busy at the lock the mate had found her own niche interest: opposite Shiplake Mill House (where previously her mother had relations and spent holidays in her youth) an old lady lived in a dilapidated gypsy caravan; a certain if disjointed sense of noblesse oblige seemed to involve the mate in her welfare, shopping and cleaning, with a quid quo pro that our precious milk could be delivered there.

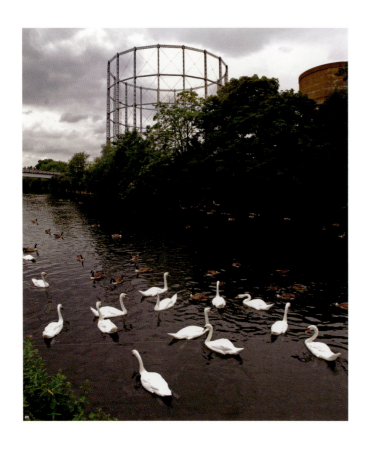

Reading

Approaching Reading in 1950, the skipper, who couldn't bear to miss a chance for an exploration, turned into the Kennet and Avon Canal. Since the canal had long been abandoned to navigation, we were clearly a spectacle, as the mate notes rather snootily: *'Passed by gas works and a mean street of tall old dwellings, watched with great interest by housewives and scoffing small boys.'*

Weeds in the water and a lack of depth meant we didn't even get the short distance to the first lock before turning round to re-run the gauntlet. In 2008 the skeleton of the gasworks remains, but the 'tall old dwellings' have given way to newly developed housing; the towpath is an urban promenade leading on to shopping precincts which celebrate the now reopened canal. The biggest hazard to navigation looks to be the large flotilla of swans.

Just upstream we moored on the wharf at Reading Bridge for supplies. Reading's real interface with the Thames is further on, at Caversham Bridge where today social and entertainment facilities rival those of a seaside resort; steadfast amongst it all is the rowing club, timeless on a summer evening training session.

'Tied to a willow above Reading for birthday tea of kippered herrings on toast and orange jelly.'

Top left: Kennet and Avon Canal;
Left: Rowing club by Caversham bridge;
Facing page: Wharf at Reading bridge.

Goring Gap

I stop at Pangbourne; it's eight o'clock in the evening but the Whitchurch bridge keeper is still taking the 20p toll from a stream of cars; below is a different world, with children learning to kayak in the quiet river, lit by shafts of late sun. I'm hoping to get a view that could define the Goring Gap where, in prehistory, the Thames cut through the chalk hills. The slopes of the Berkshire Downs drop down to the river from the west and the Chiltern Hills rise up on the other side, the steep slopes softened by dense woodland.

I move on to Streatley where the bridge does provide me with a viewpoint. The sound of rushing water follows me, for nowhere have I seen so many weirs spread around the riverscape; on the Goring side adjacent to the lock the final swirl and gurgle is from the race of an old moss-covered mill.

The red kite has been re-introduced into the wild on the high ridge of the Chilterns and as a result these magnificent birds are a frequent sight over the reaches of the river around Goring.

Top: Dovecot, Goring Mill;
Above: Red kite;
Facing page: Goring Gap.

With the Environment Agency

A week later I am back in Goring, heading downstream in an Environment Agency launch, named *Seven Springs*. Up and down the river from Lechlade to Teddington patrol boats are constantly monitoring the river usage, checking on license evasion, speeding and any other infringement. Matt Strange and Steve Miles have an official brief – to make a 'speed and wash' check on Pangbourne School's new catamaran coaching boats; I'm glad to see they have binoculars with them as I'm hoping we'll spot *Sir Humphrey*.

At Pangbourne Richard Follet (an international rower who is today involved in the England junior squad coaching and management) is in charge of the school boats. Matt unpacks his speed camera and Steve his measuring stick to check the level of wash. The school's new boats disturb the river so little that at 25 km/hour Steve can hardly measure it; they easily pass the EA test and as a result they can display the all-important blue pennant which shows they are, while 'working', exempt from the river's blanket 8 km/hour speed limit. The wash a boat causes is a function of the shape of its hull as well as the water pushed out by the propellor. These tiny catamarans (they come from Shanghai, a product of Chinese development for the 2008 Olympic Games) look a little like pedalos, but are based on hulls as slim as rowing eights, while the thrust from the propellor of the outboard is contained between the two hulls. The school will have eight of them – a measure of how many boats and crews they have training, and how seriously they defend their reputation for excellence in the sport.

At Mapledurham, I don't need binoculars to notice *Lazy Days* (see page 13), a Dunkirk veteran, but sadly not *Sir Humphrey*. While Matt has been with me out on the weir, Steve has picked up an extra crew member to bring our launch down through the lock. Lauren Hine is summer assistant lock keeper, a job she has done previously in her long summer breaks from Glasgow art school. So did she want to be a lock keeper? I ask her. The answer: not enough money. Perhaps she'll have to be a famous artist.

Downstream from Reading bridge we arrive at the EA jetty and boathouse. Inside, two launches are half under wraps after a day of varnishing and polishing so as to show their best face, *de rigeur*, at Henley Regatta; the agency is in charge of river traffic and will have six boats on duty.

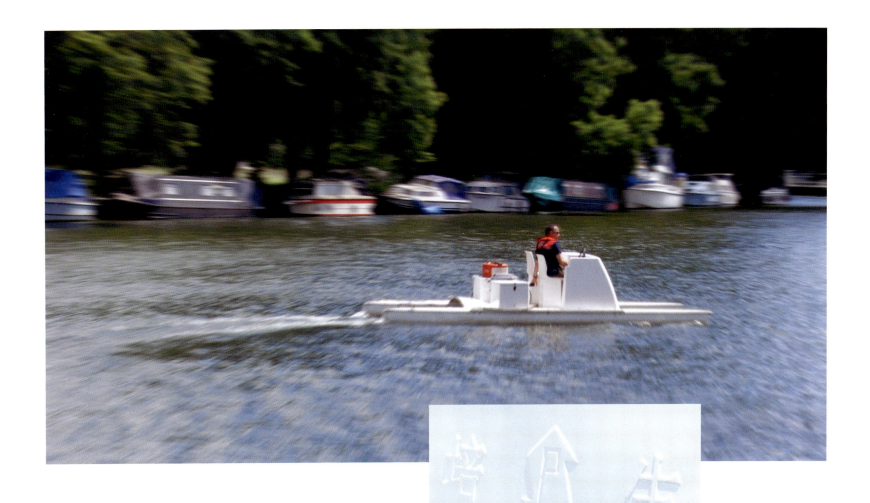

Top: Richard Follet tests Pangbourne School's new coaching catamaran; Inset: The catamaran's Shanghai logo. Left: Lauren Hine, assistant lock keeper.

Facing page, left: Matt Strange and Steve Miles of the Environment Agency measure the speed and wash of the new boat; Right: Richard Follett receives the all-important blue pennants.

Goring and Streatley Regatta

A hundred years ago every town and village on the upper Thames had its own regatta. Today the only two to stay close to Henley in their competitiveness, Marlow and Wallingford, have moved their events to the purpose-built rowing lake at Eton; almost all the regatta days on the Thames now feature light-hearted fun races, many with 'dragon boats'.

The twin villages of Goring and Streatley hold just such a regatta, with an atmosphere as formal as a village fete. In fact it *is* a village fete, with funfair, band stand and stalls. The difference is that it takes place on the meadows beside the beautiful reach above Cleeve Lock and the river features large, with a mixture of racing fours and eights as well as enter-on-the-day family canoe racing. Goring and Streatley has a proud history,with an extensive and valuable collection of trophies dating back to the 1880s (when serious contenders like London and Thames rowing clubs won their Grand Challenge cup). The regatta never got going again following the First World War, until 1995, when a band of enthusiasts brought it back to life so successfully that I could count almost five hundred cars in their car park.

Goring and Streatley embraced my photo idea with enthusiasm; with not a blazer in sight we could celebrate the spirit of the day (and what the photograph doesn't show is the willingness with which they moved all the cups from the prize-giving marquee onto the back of the timing barge, and back, just to suit me).

Above: Confusion at the start of a family canoe race;
Facing page: Goring and Streatley trophies with, left to right, Tim Gill, Brian Barnes and Hedley West.

Consuta and Sam Saunders

There is one more steamer I was keen to see, *Consuta*, built as an umpire's launch in 1898. Her design was in response to a brief from Henley Royal Regatta for rapid acceleration and high speed with minimal wash. Her 'tunnel' stern, the propellor and rudder housed in an inverted semicircular sectioned trough, helped control the wash; the key to acceleration was light weight, achieved by a new, previously untried hull construction. Four layers of mahogany veneer were sandwiched with calico and fixed with copper stitching (there were no waterproof glues at the time). This patented method became widely adopted and was called Consuta Ply.

After a variety of owners in the early twentieth century, *Consuta* had her steam engine removed in 1923; presumably with an internal combustion engine fitted, she went on with her umpiring duties until 1960. New owners in 1975 began a restoration programme and in 1998 a trust was formed: heritage lottery money enabled this long process to come to fruition at Kew Steam Museum and at Henwood and Dean's Hambleden boatyard, with steam trials taking place in 2001. Now *Consuta* is based at Beale Park; Brian Smith, chairman of the trust, ensures that she is regularly steamed up for outings, such as the one I go to see – for a group of Kew Steam Museum supporters taking a ride down the river to Pangbourne.

Above:Brian Smith, skipper of Consuta, *stoking coal; Right: Springfield Yard slipway. Facing page:* Consuta *near Beale Park.*

Consuta was built by Sam Saunders in his Springfield Yard, upstream from Cleeve lock. His speciality was speedboats, and he tested them on the long straight reach up to Benson, clandestinely as even then there was a speed limit on the river. One night a particularly fast run caused so much wash that a group of camping skiffs moored at The Leathern Bottel capsized, decanting the sleeping crews into the river. Sam Saunders abandoned Springfield in 1916 to concentrate on his other yard on the Isle of Wight. He later formed a partnership with A.V. Roe to develop flying boats, and later hovercraft.

Springfield's future is to be a nature reserve. Hidden from the river by trees, the remains of the yard are represented by the winch and slipway, where lengths of Brunel's re-used broad-gauge track still sit in place amongst rampant vegetation. And incidentally, The Leathern Bottel is not a pub but a very upmarket restaurant, so don't expect to call in for a pleasant riverside drink.

Above: Dinghy with 'skipper' and crew, Littlestoke ferry, 1947; Below: Flowers commemorate a tragedy at Littlestoke ferry; Facing page: Brunel's Stoke viaduct.

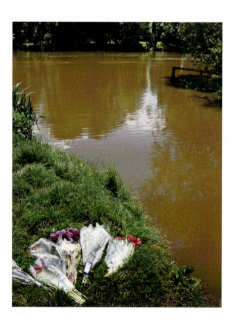

Littlestoke and Cholsey

Back upstream, Brunel's Bristol railway has stayed with the river through the Goring Gap. Crossing twice at Gatehampton and South Stoke, it then finally leaves the river, heading west towards Didcot. A mile further on, in 1947 *Sir Humphrey* moored up at the old Littlestoke ferry site. Our neighbour from home, Mrs Hancock, had just moved to Cholsey and we planned to stay a few days. The following afternoon we rowed across to what looks more like an old ford than a ferry wharf, walked up the lane for a mile to take tea in her garden at Broadlands. A flavour of 1940s life is provided by the mate: '*Mrs Hancock helped by introducing us to the trades people.*' This proved to be less than efficacious for an entry two days later sadly recalls: '*an hour's wait for one and a half pounds of biscuits*'. Remembering that rationing was still in force, perhaps it was the difficulties of supplies ('*tinned milk, tinned rabbit*') that drove us on the short river trip to Wallingford. The skipper again demonstrated his maverick tendencies by mooring up at the Salter's Steamers jetty (a bit like parking a car in the bus stop): '*had to be back in half an hour as the steamer was due.*'

We obviously had a social time at Littlestoke, with friends and family congregating in Mrs H's garden, and decamping to the river; entertainment seems to have been provided by the railway – '*boys wonderful time as the trains pass right by the garden*' – and a trip to see Brunel's handiwork is also deemed worthy of mention: '*sixteen aboard to visit the viaduct – anxious moments as skipper righted an engine fault.*'

I visit Cholsey but fail to find the garden by the railway. The small bay where the track terminates at the ferry crossing to Littlestoke, where our dinghy is beached in the mate's 1948 photo, is overtaken by high water in June 2008. Bunches of flowers strewn on the bank, and cards with sad short requiems, testify to the mortal danger of the power of a river in flood.

46

Medieval Bridges

Wallingford, Abingdon, and Culham in between, can all boast medieval bridges. Wallingford had been the more important town, with the lowest all-season ford, but Abingdon was the first to build a stone bridge in the fifteenth century. Wallingford quickly followed suit. Both bridges have seen serious changes over the centuries but they both retain original work with pointed gothic arches in evidence amongst the more recent round topped alterations.

Culham is just downstream from Abingdon on what was once the old river course; this is now a backwater, crossed by a pair of road bridges. The older bridge, now not used, without the pressures of road or river traffic has retained its unaltered medieval structure.

These three ancient structures are not the oldest on the Thames – they are west of Oxford at Newbridge and Radcot (see page 70).

Above: Blue plaque, Culham;
Below: Culham Old Bridge;
Facing page: Wallingford Bridge.

Wallingford and Wittenham Clumps

It is easy to couple Wallingford and Abingdon, for they have a lot in common as well as their old bridges: placed on the south-west bank of the Thames, some twenty and ten miles downstream from Oxford, both have ancient charters and have been powerful centres of trade since the twelfth century. Wallingford's importance could be measured by the fact that in the thirteenth century it had its own mint and no fewer than ten churches.

Both towns, like Oxford, sided with the Royalists in the Civil War and both suffered setbacks at the hands of Oliver Cromwell, Wallingford losing its castle as a result. Wallingford remains well known for its rowing; it can boast the longest between-locks stretch on the upper river, but the annual regatta now takes place on the purpose-built rowing lake at Eton.

The mate was very keen on the landmark hill topped with a grove of trees known as Wittenham Clumps, downstream from Clifton Hampden. She may have thought it looked a good walk, or she may have been attracted to it by its association with the surrealist painter Paul Nash (First World War artist and friends with Moore and Hepworth) whose younger brother John, an artist too, she had known growing up in Princes Risborough. So while staying at Clifton Hampden in 1952, 'for a treat' we mounted an expedition, over the bridge and along the lanes picking wild flowers and moaning in turn, the mate taking a long scenic route so as to visit the pretty village of Long Wittenham on the way. I remember impressive views from the hilltop, but also relief at the prospect of a shorter way home, dropping quickly back into Little Wittenham for cold drinks. I acted as diarist that day: '*over the river footbridge to Day's lock where we had to buy penny tickets to use the bridge over the weir.*' Now I'm back at Day's Lock to photograph the first steamer of the season coming upriver, with the iconic hill in the background. "Cross over the weir bridge if you want to," the lock keeper told me; perhaps with a long memory he added: "It is free".

Top left: Rowing eight, downsteam from Wallingford Bridge;
Left: Wallingford Castle remains; Facing page: Wittenham Clumps
from Day's Lock.

Abingdon

Early in the fifteenth century Abingdon entered a period of prosperity, largely driven by its abbey and the wool trade. With the coming of the industrial revolution it hit a new surge of trading success with the building of a lock on the river in 1790 and the opening of the Wilts & Berks canal in 1810.

There is not much left of its old abbey but the town retains a thriving unspoilt centre, paying tribute to all those centuries of change. Between Abingon and Wallingford are several picturesque villages – Benson, today busy with boat hire, Shillingford, Little Wittenham and Dorchester, with a ruined abbey of its own. The upstream voyages of *Sir Humphrey* saw us choose none of these settlements as our base, but the tiny village of Clifton Hampden.

Bottom left: Abbey dovecot, Abingdon;
Below: County Hall; Facing page:
Entrance to the Wilts & Berks Canal.

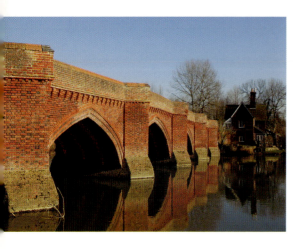

Clifton Hampden

En route for Oxford in 1948 we ran aground at Clifton Hampden and then spent the night anchored below the church on its high bluff. In the morning we surveyed the village with its pretty cottages and a convenient bridge, moved across to moor on the far bank by a small bathing beach, and liked it so much we adopted it as a favourite spot.

We returned many times, often for a week or more with the skipper making only occasional appearances, cycling to and fro while working in High Wycombe. As well as seeming a perfect mooring, Clifton Hampden had the mate's favourite church; after a sunday service her diary almost always referred to the theme of the sermon, so that scattered amongst the frequent references to tinned sausages and 'condemned' (condensed) milk comes 'Blessed are they that hunger and thirst after righteousness.'

Actually we tended to thirst after fresh milk and as Sir Humphrey had no fridge (indeed, we didn't have one at home) we were 'very lucky to find a milkman ... said we could have a pint each day – more than we could have hoped for with our emergency ration cards.' Daily trips to the village shop were the norm, but the cards were an ongoing problem: 'Walked to Dorchester and bought ration of chops. Neither of two grocers could sell us bacon as it was not available on our emergency card.' We only walked once – after that it was a steamer to Day's Lock and then a short stride across the meadows. Unfortunately Wallingford and Abingdon were tantalisingly out of reach, for rather like some rural bus services today, the timing of the steamers sometimes meant you could get there but not back.

Today Clifton Hampden seems unchanged – the church on its high bluff, the tiny shop up the lane and the line of cottages set back from the river behind the winter boardwalk. It's early summer and something I don't remember from 1950 is the yellow rape, colonising the flood meadows on both sides of the river – very colourful but probably to be regretted.

Clifton Hampden has one more much loved and much feted feature, the Barley Mow, which Jerome K. Jerome in Three Men in a Boat describes as 'without exception the quaintest most old-world inn up the river'. By walking over the distinctive red brick bridge (by the famous architect George Gilbert Scott – built with ornate detailing and pointed arches in deference to the medieval bridge work of the monks up- and downstream), we could have enjoyed the hospitality of one of the Thames' most famous inns – but we didn't; despite the modern perception of river holidays being a watery pub crawl, we almost never indulged.

Perhaps the mate had a wry sense of what might have been, for when we finally left Clifton Hampden for the last time in 1953 she wrote, rather as a regretful epitaph: '*Here's a health to the Barley Mow, me boys … with a nipperkin, pipperkin and the brown bowl. A health to the Barley Mow.*' I don't know where she got that from, but in the spirit of making up for lost time (nearly sixty years), I'm at last making a visit. The original timber-framed and thatched cruck-house has '1352' painted on its white render; the interior, extended to cope with the summer surge of visitors, is everything an old country inn is expected to be. In gilded lettering, suitably smoke-stained, though probably only Edwardian in origin, a rather amusing couplet claims 'Hops, Turkey, Carp and Beer, all arrived in the same year – 1520'. No bets on the veracity of either date.

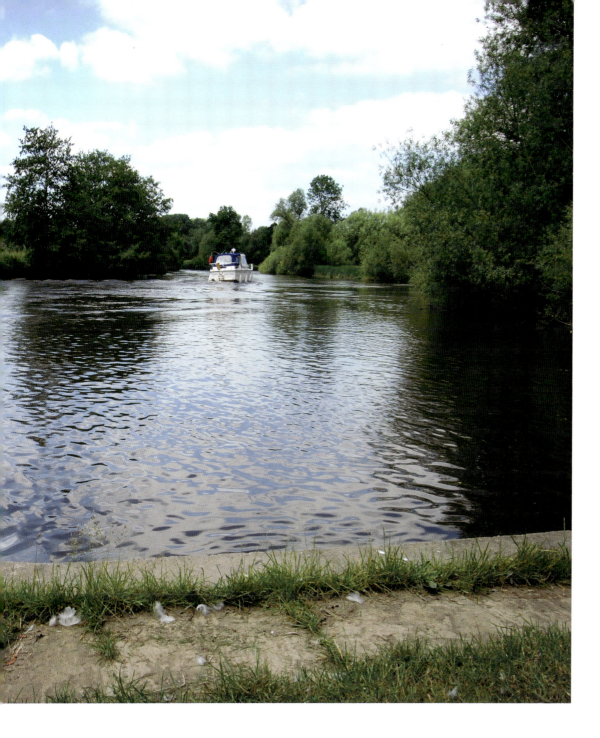

Above: Locked gate and signs at Shillingford;
Left: Shillingford Wharf.

Oxford

My memories of travelling through Oxford as a child on *Sir Humphrey* are quite blank, perhaps wiped out by subsequent experiences. The responsibilities of holding on to a rope against the rushing sluice of water in Sandford lock, the deepest on the river, are directly followed by being moored up north of the city at Godstow. In fact Sandford nearly created a catastrophe, for up front my elder brother's rope broke and he did well to loop the remnant around a bollard and hold on. Later Godstow provided its own drama.

The mate's diary tells more than I remembered: *'we moored by the university barges, C identifying them from his postcard of the college crests.'* These 'barges', heavy and squat but elegantly decorated with ornate carved superstructures and balconies proudly displaying their college coats of arms, famously lined the north bank on the long reach leading past Christchurch Meadow. Their spacious interiors were clubrooms and housed the racing eights, while their roofs provided viewing platforms for the races. Three remain in Oxford. One by Port Meadow is used as a houseboat, as is *Corpus Christi*, moored up a muddy creek near Donnington Bridge. The third, still belonging to St John's College, provides a hospitality suite for a hotel at Sandford. Their original function has been taken on by a line of modern boathouses with club rooms and balconies above.

Approaching Oxford, just before Donnington Bridge, is the workshop and slipway of the famous Salter's Steamers. This listed building might look quiet but inside is a hive of activity: every winter every 'steamer' in the Salter's fleet comes out of the water for inspection, repair or improvements.

Top left: Reading is given a winter overhaul;
Centre left: Salter's slipway;
Left: Corpus Christi barge, Donnington Bridge;
Facing page: St John's barge, Sandford.

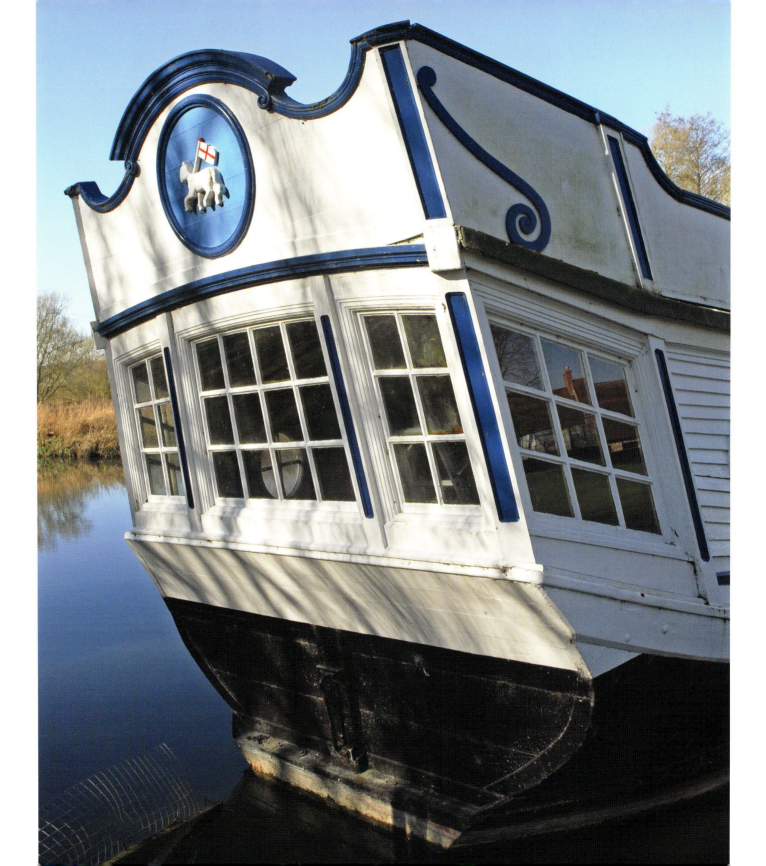

Above: Steamers at their winter
mooring on Christchurch Meadow;
Below: Folly Bridge.

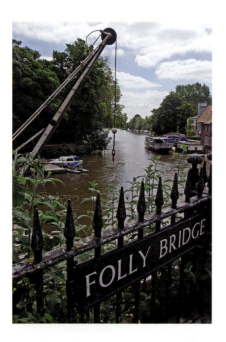

Salter's Steamers

Upstream of the college boathouses (we'll take a look at the rowing on the next page), past Christchurch meadow Oxford proper is announced by Folly Bridge, which carries the old main road from the south into the city.

As well as its ancient origin (a bridge on this site since the twelfth century), Folly Bridge has another particular strand of history. Opposite The Head of the River pub is the office of Salter's, whose claim to fame is their fleet of river steamers. In the 1950s these handsome vessels, all named after river towns and villages (*Wargrave, Sonning, Reading,* etc.) ran downstream to Windsor and beyond to a regular timetable – like a bus service – stopping for passengers at locks and at tiny rural jetties. At every lock a long blast of their steam hooter announced their approach to ensure priority over the waiting queue of small craft.

Here is a modern story to tell just what a lasting impression the Salter's steamers could make. A year before starting on this book, by chance I took the towpath walk from Iffley Lock to Folly Bridge with a friend. Rounding a bend I saw some three hundred yards ahead the distinctive outline of two steamers, still familiar after five decades. I told my friend of this impressive fleet, with their handsome profile and sleek cutaway 'counter' sterns, with just two exceptions which were high round-ended (technically 'tunnel' stern – see page 44). The pair in view included one of these variants: "I expect that first one is named *Mapledurham,*"I ventured. His scorn turned to wonder as we approached close enough to read the nameplate, and I was amazed too at such a strong sixty-year memory (and by my 50 per cent luck!)

I visit the office at Folly Bridge and, to my surprise and pleasure, discover that not much has changed. True, steam is replaced with diesel power, but there is still a timetable serving the river villages and in the summer the boats go as far down river as Staines.

In 2008 Salter's is celebrating its 150th anniversary. Best known for their 'steamer' operation, in their early years they were boatbuilders and had strong connections with the university. As well as providing the boat clubs with their lightweight racing eights, at the other end of the scale they also supplied the college 'barges' from their Folly Bridge yard. In 1949 this included a chandlery: '*took a penny ferry from Christchurch meadow to get new rope from Salters – met with surprise that skipper could splice it himself.*' In those days the company still had the use of a complex of buildings on the site, including what is today the Head of the River pub (at the back of which they still hire out skiffs and punts).

Above: Paul and John Salter of Salter's Steamers, at Folly Bridge.

John Salter is honoured to be one of the twenty-four Royal Watermen; this ceremonial title involves dressing in an outfit similar to the red and gold of the Beefeaters, but calls for active duty as bodyguard to the Queen, or other members of the royal family, when they are using boats on the river. The firm's joint founder, John H. Salter, was for twenty-four years chairman of the Boat Trades Association, and was awarded the framed deed that his descendant, today's John Salter, proudly displays – he and his son Paul are the fifth and sixth generation in the firm. The list of previous BTA chairmen contains many names that remain familiar on the Thames – Wood, Turk, Hobbs, Ayling – which reiterates the continuity which seems such a strong feature of the river.

Oxford – rowing

A decade after looking at that postcard of college crests, during my first week up at Balliol I was back on the same stretch of river as a crowd of us 'freshers' were testing out for Oxford's most renowned sport. Most of the chaps were from 'boaty' public schools. A coach with a cap and blazer asked me if I had done any rowing. I told him: yes, since I was five years old, in a dinghy. He pulled down the peak of his cap and turned away to hide a smirk, but put me into a training boat fixed firmly to the edge – a 'bank-tub' – using an oar with a hole in the blade. "See how you get on with this little dinghy."

I spent an hour trying to row the bank from Oxford to Iffley. "If you want to row you'll be down here every afternoon," Peaky then told me. What about rugby and running? I dared ask. "No chance: you row or you don't. See you tomorrow." Could I decide to forgo running on Iffley Road, Roger Bannister's sub-four-minute-mile track? Regrettably, I never went back to the towpath.

But now here I am, and how things have changed. All the training takes place in a gym so bank tubs are a thing of the past; as is the notion of men's colleges. The women's captain, Maya Bahoshy, brought her crew for a coxed four along to the boathouse to meet me. "This is not necessarily the final team," she claimed. "Everyone fights for places." As they lowered their boat into the water I noticed that their four personal pairs of trainers were screwed down to the floor of the boat, but I supposed that would not be allowed to influence the selection process.

Above: The Balliol girls' eight on the way to the start of a race; Right: Balliol crew members outside the boathouse.

In May I am back again to watch the third day of 'Summer Eights', a four-day competition where all the colleges enter men's and women's crews, and some second and third boats too, in 'divisions' of twelve; there are seven men's divisions and six women's. The course runs from below Donnington Bridge to Folly Bridge, but this isn't a race to a finish line. Starting simultaneously but a length and a half apart, the aim is to catch the boat ahead (known as a 'bump' but usually a non-physical overlap), after which both pull to one side and stop. I ask the umpire who decides if there is a 'bump' and he tells me the overtaken cox simply raises his arm to concede. Sporting tradition rules.

Both of Balliol's first crews are in their top divisions: I find that the four women I photographed are split up – only two made it to the first boat, which does really well, moving from eighth to fifth over the four days. It is Balliol's men that are the real stars though: they have bumped each of the two preceding days and are starting as 'Head of the River', and remain unbeaten on days three and four.

Right: Balliol men's eight, almost out of sight, heading the first division; in their wake, Magdalen are about to be 'bumped' by Oriel; in the foreground, Christ Church are about to catch Pembroke.

Port Meadow and Godstow

Moving upstream from Folly Bridge the river divides, and also sees off the Oxford Canal north on its way to join the complex inland waterway network of the Midlands. The Thames then passes alongside Port Meadow, expansive flood plain for the river and summer playground for North Oxford. Just above Godstow lock we moored *Sir Humphrey* by the historic ruins of Godstow Nunnery. The mate had friends to visit in Wolvercote with a tale to tell from the 1947 flood: *'It was very exciting as they had boats and swans up and down the road – they cooked sunday dinner standing in eight inches of water.'* We were to suffer our own drama that night: *'checking the mooring ropes the skipper found we'd blown right across the river'*, – a scare I do remember, finding ourselves adrift in the dark only fifty yards above the weir. *'Anchor, then roped onto a bush – a difficult night in alarming wind.'*

As well as enjoying the hospitality of the famous Trout Inn, before heading upstream from Godstow it is worth a walk into Wytham to the village shop. Long empty stretches of river lie ahead and there will be no other chance for supplies until you reach the head of navigation at Lechlade.

Above: The Trout Inn, Godstow;
Top right: Remains of Godstow Nunnery;
Right: Port Meadow.

Ferries, fords and bridges

Upstream from Godstow the Thames enters a sparsely populated rural landscape of tiny hamlets for some thirty miles. When you finally arrive at Lechlade, this small sleepy Cotswold town seems a metropolis compared with anything in between.

The river makes slow progress in gently meandering loops, and its 'valley', as flat as the fens, is apparently limitless with no hills visible on either side. Across this wide expanse boats appear in the distance with indeterminate direction and no reference to the river itself, their superstructures seeming to float disembodied over the water meadows. This empty riverscape is punctuated by an occasional farmers' bridge and old ford and ferry sites. River crossings have always been important points for financial and, in times of dispute, strategic reasons. The existence of fords is easily demonstrated by the names of the settlements – Shillingford, Sandford, Oxford, Duxford. These gradually gave way to ferries and then to bridges. In the mid-twentieth century there were still several ferries running (the mate notes: '*Bablock Hythe – emergency stop as the rope for the ferry is spotted stretched across the river*') but mostly today they are a memory. In fact at Bablock Hythe it is still possible, in theory, to arrange a crossing; however in the spring of 2008 the ferryboat remains on the edge of the pub car park where it was washed to in the floods of July 2007.

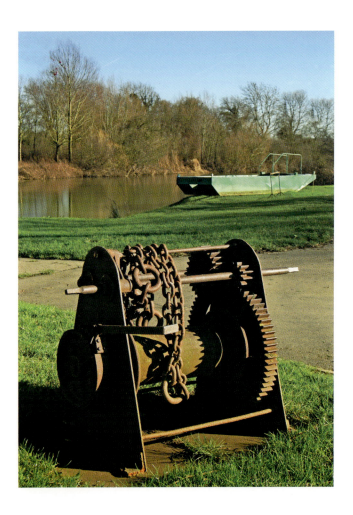

Top: Toll bridge, Eynsham;
Left: The ferry, Bablock Hythe;
Facing page: The ford, Duxford.

Newbridge and the Windrush

Approaching Newbridge, the calm of the empty landscape is broken as a rush of modernity intervenes, with the Witney to Abingdon road crossing the river. The bridge is flanked by two pubs, both with tellingly large car parks, The Rose Revived and the Maybush (an apt name in mid-May when blackthorn blossom covers the surrounding hedgerows like thick fallen snow).

Above the bridge the Thames is joined by a significant tributary, the Windrush. This is the considerable stream you can't help noticing decorating the idyllic Cotswold valley to the north of the main Oxford to Cheltenham road; indeed, it has travelled through two counties to reach Newbridge, rising at a height of over two hundred metres just south of Broadway (certainly higher than the Thames, and longer, possibly even than the Churn as well – see page 80). I'll admit I didn't know of this stream as a boy on *Sir Humphrey*, but I knew the name. The Thames Conservancy (the river authority of the time) ran a fleet of launches, each of which bore the name of a Thames tributary – *Evenlode*, *Kennet* and so on, including, I believe, *Windrush*. Rather surprisingly, today's authority, the Environment Agency, still run a fleet, and they still have tributary names (though sadly no *Windrush*). But this name reminds me now of an altogether different ship.

The same year that the skipper brought *Sir Humphrey* up the Thames from Kingston to Bourne End, an ex-German troop-carrier, *Monte Rosa*, was taken from Kiel to Glasgow for a refit and (never mind risking bad luck) given a new name: *Empire Windrush*. The following year it made an historic voyage from Kingston (this one in Jamaica), taking a month to reach Tilbury on the tidal Thames. The five hundred West Indians on board were the first of many arriving to take on one of the low-paid jobs which couldn't be filled in Britain's post-war economy.

For many of these immigrants who had been in the armed services it was a return to England; other arrivals were keen to visit, and perhaps settle in, the 'mother country'. A large number of the 1948 arrivals to London were temporarily housed in a wartime bomb shelter, part of Clapham South underground station. As they moved on to find accommodation and jobs they naturally gravitated to the nearest labour exchange, sited in Coldharbour Lane, Brixton, starting the trend to this area becoming a strongly West Indian neighbourhood.

Back in a more rural part of the Thames Valley in 1948 I was a small boy in my first year at school; going home for lunch I was getting on or off a number 35 bus in the station yard four times a day, ideally placed to see the express trains from Paddington as they paused for breath at High Wycombe. At midday the *Cambrian Coast Express* was on its way to Aberystwyth and Pwllelli, but even more impressive was the morning *Inter City* which really made a country boy feel his town was on the map – from Paddington to Wolverhampton, stopping only at Wycombe and Birmingham. Local legend had it that this little town of furniture factories acquired its very early, and apparently disproportionate, population of West Indians in the early fifties as immigrants boarded the train at Birmingham and got off at the first stop!

Urban myths notwithstanding there must be an almost unimaginable gulf between the realities of Britain, the promised land, that the *Empire Windrush* travellers experienced on arrival in South London and the rich rural landscapes of the Windrush, whose tumbling flow so prettily enhances the well-heeled Cotswolds, exemplified by that archetypal tourist village, Bourton-on-the-Water.

Top: Plaque commemorating the Empire Windrush, *Tilbury; Left: The Windrush at Bourton-on-the-Water; Facing page: The Windrush joins the Thames at Newbridge.*

Thurrock Heritage

Empire Windrush arrives at Tilbury Landing Stage 22nd June 1948

The iconic arrival of the first post-war migration of West-Indians to Great Britain. Lord Kitchener sings live 'London that's the place for me'.

By Thames to all Peoples of the World

Newbridge and Radcot

Back to the Thames it is worth noticing the ancient bridges at Newbridge and at Radcot. The next main road crossing upstream, Radcot is rich in history and is a popular rural destination thanks to the Swan Inn, but is too small to be marked on a road atlas. Both bridges claim to be the oldest on the river: Newbridge concedes that Radcot was built first (1220), and the basis for its own claim is that Radcot's central arch has been altered, and that the channel it crosses has become a backwater.

The history of Radcot's bridge includes an incident in 1387: the central one of three arches was dismantled by Henry Bolingbroke (later Henry IV) to trap supporters of Richard II. When the bridge was rebuilt two years later it was given a round-topped arch. The ribbing under the pointed gothic arches of both bridges is a strong pointer to the original builders,

probably monks from the Priory of St John the Baptist at Lechlade (who, upstream, were also responsible for the original St John's Bridge, also dated around 1220). In fact the ribbing appears to be decorative not structural; in a recent accident at Newbridge, a misguided narrowboat knocked away a section of stone which proved to have been only lightly attached to the arch.

The river at Radcot has two natural courses; the southern one passes under the old bridge, while to the north an equally ancient bridge was replaced using iron girders in 1863. In the meadow beyond, the suggestion that a multiplicity of banks, ditches and depressions concealed a system of Saxon wharves was recently confirmed by a BBC *Time Team* archaeological dig. Between these two courses a new 'navigation' channel was cut in association with canal building – see page 72.

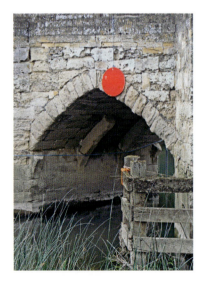

All river crossings have a strategic significance at times of disturbance: during the Civil War, when Oxford was a Royalist stronghold, this is underlined by the well documented record of skirmishes around all the bridges up- and downstream of the city. The importance of the bridges, and the river as a defensive line, also comes right into modern times. All along the upper Thames during the Second World War concrete 'pillboxes' were built into the agricultural landscape to defend the river crossings against a possible German invasion. As a desperate final move, every bridge was mined with explosives to enable it to be destroyed in the face of an enemy advance. These plans for demolition were in the hands of the army; local farmer John Willmer was a corporal in the Home Guard whose responsibilities were defence, day-by-day watches and checks at the bridge.

With the loan of a dinghy from the Swan Inn, I row John round to the old channel so he can show me the ancient bridge and a pillbox close by. Back in the pub garden he told me of those dark days in 1940: of two-hour-on and two-hour-off watches through the night based in a chicken shed, and of challenging everyone crossing the bridge ("The only trouble we had was with RAF men driving back to base from the cinema in Farringdon – they soon showed their papers when a loaded Lee Enfield rifle was poked into the car window"). He remembered learning to use the Sten gun and the Bren gun, going on a course with the SAS – how to use a knife in

*Above: John Willmer at
Radcot Bridge;*

*Facing page: World War
Two pillbox, Radcot, and
damaged gothic arch,
Newbridge.*

hand-to-hand fighting – and how secret everything was supposed to be. "We didn't know where the orders were coming from, so we couldn't give anything away under torture." I ask him jokingly if that hadn't mean running the risk of obeying the wrong people – and he agrees. "Secrecy was the most important thing of all."

It is impossible not to think of the television sitcom *Dad's Army* and believe that for all the humour it was probably rather close to the truth. John Willmer had wanted to join the RAF but was told to stay working on his farm. He was twenty years old in 1940, a young man in an old men's platoon – think of the 'Pike', character. However, as the owner of what he nostalgically calls a 'shooting brake' ("Would that be an estate car, John?" – "No, perhaps a station wagon") he was the platoon's driver, just like Corporal Jones. As he talks of the war, sounding uncannily like Jones, I am lulled into a three-way reverie: listening to this old man's tales, watching 1968 television with the skipper and thinking of the nightmare that defending England against the storm troopers would have been.

Top: Brian Lukehurst at Friars Court
moorings: Above: John Hall, pollarding
willows.

Radcot and Friars Court

The opening of the Thames & Severn Canal, linking Gloucester to the river at Lechlade, brought a huge increase in traffic on the upper reaches. Narrowboats coming downstream couldn't easily negotiate the tight corner leading into Radcot's ancient bridge and in 1787 the new middle channel, with its typical high round-arched bridge, was cut specifically for them by the canal company. The present pub garden, on this 'navigation' channel, was a commercial river wharf where stone coming overland from Taynton quarry was loaded en route to build St Paul's Cathedral (a claim also made at Newbridge, where it is said it was floated down the Windrush on rafts). The new wharf, combined with the lock on this channel, put the ancient wharves to the north out of business and made the old southern stream a backwater.

Friars Court, a 600-acre farm sited one mile up the Witney road, was bought by the Willmer family in 1917. John Wilmer was born four years later and in 2008, at the age of 87, is still actively managing the land with the help of his son Charles. John is a remarkable man: a devotion to traditional ways might be expected from one born so early in the last century, but what seems unusual is the way he seamlessly blends the old country habits with modernism. "In 1995 my banker asked me why I didn't go into the 'leisure business'. I told my late wife Frances what he'd said and she told me – 'Well, get on with it then' – so I did." The farm now hosts educational trips, a visitors' tea room, wedding receptions and the stone buildings in the yard include a gymnasium. On the riverbank by The Swan there is a caravan park and thirty berths for holiday cruisers.

Meanwhile John is a passionate advocate of the traditional activities that fit in with this riverside location, encouraging rush-cutting and willow-pollarding. Trees are cut in early spring, at head height to prevent cattle grazing on the fresh shoots which immediately sprout. Harvested on a five-year cycle, pollarding produces branches as thick as a man's arm, traditionally used for fence posts, but today fuelling John's woodburning stoves. Government-sponsored schemes have led him to experiment with plantations of willow for a second method of renewable growth – the so-called 'short rotation'. Trees are coppiced (cut at ground level) every year, producing finger-thick lengths for fence- or hurdle-making. When there is no demand for hurdle-making (sadly, frequently), the 'green' cut shoots are 'chipped' and burned as bio-mass fuel in nearby Didcot power station.

Above: Tony and Kate Handley harvesting rushes.

Cutting rushes has a double benefit: it keeps the river clear and it provides the raw material for chair seats. Every summer Tony and Kate Handley come from Wantage with their boats, and family and friends, to harvest supplies for their furniture business (*rusheats.co.uk*), welcomed by John, who is keen on the continuity of this timeless tradition.

Country style even flavours the way the caravan and boat sites are managed. Many years ago Brian Lukehurst took a caravan for the summer. John liked Brian's manner and he has been back with his family every subsequent summer, bartering the season's rent for the duty of running the site. "Brian is an ex-sea captain," John told me. "Being in charge suits him – it isn't a chore but a pleasure for him."

*Above: Inglesham Church;
Right: William Morris's
house, Hammersmith.*

*Facing page: Kelmscot
Manor, screened by rushes.*

William Morris at Kelmscot

William Morris, pivotal figure of the Arts and Craft Movement, might not have approved of John Willmer's war stories, but would surely have empathised with his devotion to the old country ways. His home, Kelmscot Manor, is a mile on from Radcot, appropriately shielded from the Thames path by a screen of rushes (a favourite material for chair seats).

Despite his anti-city stance he also had a riverside home in Hammersmith and is said to have rowed his family upstream from door to door. Appalled at the Victorian vogue for ham-fisted improvements, Morris was instrumental in the restoration of the beautiful little medieval church at Inglesham *('a little gem')* three miles upstream.

Lechlade

St John's lock is the highest on the river; it boasts a statue of Old Father Thames (see page 28) and, a surprise after all the twisting through the water meadows, a straight reach with a view ahead to the spire of Lechlade church.

On our first long trip upstream in *Sir Humphrey* we spent the night moored at this charming Cotswold village. This was as far upriver as cabin cruisers go, but that didn't curtail the ambition of the skipper. In the morning we set off upstream and after half a mile passed the entrance to the derelict Thames & Severn Canal, marked by the associated Roundhouse. At this point the River Coln also joins the river and the Thames, without the benefit of the Coln's water, immediately changes from a navigable river to something not much more than a large stream. *Sir Humphrey* slowed down. "We'll see how far we can go" said the skipper. Not far. There was so little water that instead of driving the boat up the river the propellor was pulling the river back past the boat, making it even shallower. Then we were stuck. Two of us were ordered into the river to push while another was in the dinghy, pulling *Sir Humphrey* like a boy-powered tug. The mate was pushing with the boat hook and the skipper, behaving more like an admiral, found time between issuing directions to gingerly use reverse gear. We gradually got free and in deeper water turned around, our exploration of the upper reaches towards Cricklade postponed for another time in a more suitable vessel.

Sir Humphrey needed more water than family cruisers designed for the Thames; coupled with the skipper's view that anything was worth a try, running aground was not at all unusual. We normally sorted ourselves out, so this 1953 entry, '*stuck on a sand bank – towed off with a tractor under direction of Kings lock-keeper*', was exceptional.

Top left: Roundhouse marking the start of the Thames & Severn Canal;
Left: Junction of the Thames and the Coln;
Facing page: St John's Lock and Lechlade church spire.

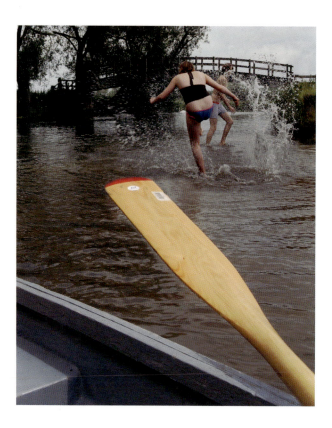

Swimming

Next time we were in Lechlade, in 1951, prudence ruled and we enjoyed the peace and solitude of these upper reaches with a punt to Hannington Bridge – 'saw nobody except reed cutters all day'. Regrettably punts are no longer available in 2008 so I am taking my kids on a rowing expedition to rediscover this tranquil scene. Upstream into a headwind it takes some effort to reach a little beach opposite the Thames & Severn Canal entrance, where we stop for a decidedly rowdy swimming and splashing session. Modern sensitivities – the children's priority is lunch – means we abort the Hannington Bridge trip; after some unprogressive rowing lessons, even downstream, we end our trip in the riverside garden of the Red Lion at Castle Eaton ('the first pub on the Thames'), sadly arriving by car, not by boat.

Before 'leisure centres' became the norm, the river towns and villages on the Thames had their own swimming pools – simply a sectioned-off area of the river itself. I particularly remember them at Hurley and Henley, but I believe they were very usual. Few people swim in the Thames today, though a heat wave in August will bring out the bathers at Port Meadow and at other camp and picnic sites. What look like a series of bright orange marker buoys are the hats of a dozen swimmers, many in wet suits, setting off from Buscot Lock for a two-day marathon to Newbridge, one of several organised by holiday firm Swimtrek every year.

Top: Swimming near Inglesham;
Above: The author's children at the Red Lion,
Castle Eaton; Right: Swimming near Hannington, 1951;
Facing page: Swimmers set off from Buscot Lock.

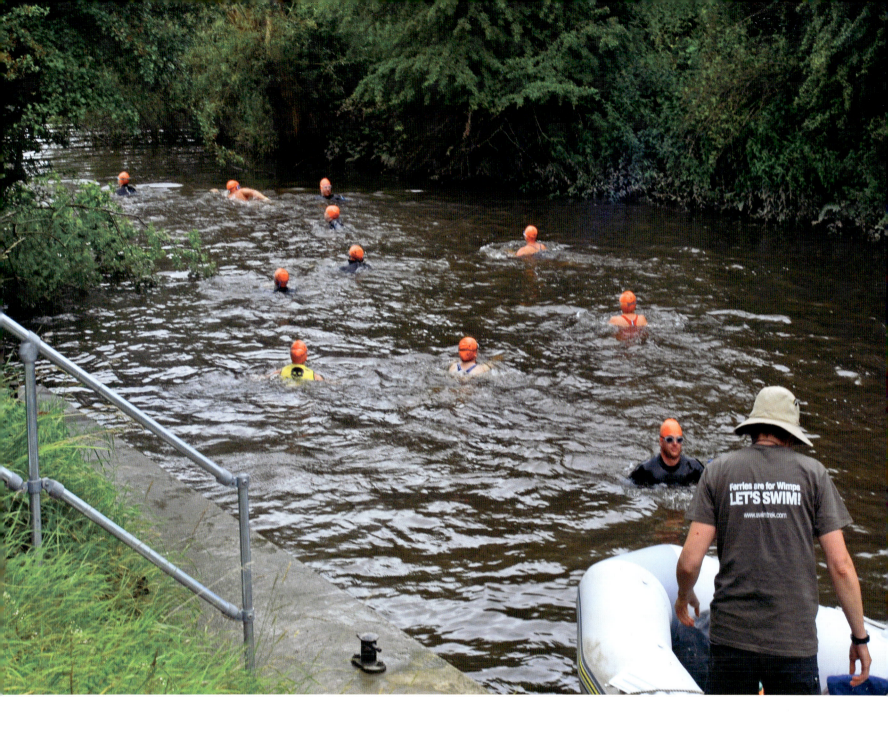

Above: Seven Springs;
Below: Blossom over the River Churn.

The Churn and Seven Springs

I'm at Cricklade in rural Gloucestershire, still a long way from the source of the river but a little confused between two rival claimants.

Growing up in the Thames Valley, amongst the gradual accretion of local wisdom was the certainty that the river flowed from a distant source in the Cotswolds called Seven Springs. Spending much time further east it was not until a recent move to West Gloucestershire, and a renewed interest in the river, that I discovered to my surprise what was at least a rival claim – the spot near to Kemble known as Thameshead. The Ordnance Survey quotes this as the source of the Thames, and Seven Springs, a dozen miles to the north, as where the River Churn rises, to join the Thames at Cricklade.

So was my childhood filled with disinformation? 'Source' is defined in a dictionary as the beginning; realistically, one would suppose that a river's source, its beginning, would be the start of its longest branch. In that case Thameshead is an impostor, for it is only about half the distance from Cricklade that Seven Springs is. Furthermore, both the Coln, which join the Thames at Lechlade, and the Windrush, at Newbridge, seem longer rivers than the stream rising at Thameshead!

At the risk of labouring the point, how can it be right for the longer stream to 'pay tribute' to the shorter? And the extraordinary fact is that the only other river I have taken serious notice of, the Severn, suffers from the same mysterious conundrum. The route to its rather vague but accepted source on the summit ridge of Plynlimon is also eclipsed by two of its 'tributaries', the rivers Vyrny and Clywedog. So when the Severn claims to be the longest river in the country, which of its streams has anyone considered? Does every river have a source chosen by historic habit rather than mapper's logic?

Facing page, top: North Meadow in flood
Below: Snake's head fritillaries.

Back to the Thames, and to the Churn: the diplomatic answer is to notice both of these claims, firstly Seven Springs, as then the Thames can be itself with no more worries. Seven Springs is just what it says – a set of seven apertures set in a stone retaining wall behind a depression next to the A436 at its junction with the A435. Water flows in all seasons, though in wet winters (and summers these days) the amount can be a gush rather than a trickle. The Churn flows prettily down its Cotswold valley, tinkling and tossing its ripples over stony rapids as it passes through the villages of Colebourne and North Cerney on its way towards Cricklade.

At North Meadow, famous for its winter floods and spring snake's head fritillaries, the Churn and the Thames flow each side before meeting on the edge of the little town.

Top: The Roundhouse Lock at Cerney Wick;
Above: Thames footpath sign;
Facing page: Swans at Clayfurlong.

Thameshead

Thameshead is situated in a field north west of the A433 road close to Kemble. For much of the year there is no water to be seen until further down the course, but heavy rain can make a spectacular scene with floods filling the meadows in the wide valley for a mile to the north. The course of the Thames is very different from that of the Churn: as Thameshead is nearly one hundred metres lower on the Cotswold ridge than Severn Springs, it runs a much more level line to Cricklade. Rather than tumbling like a mountain stream, it runs slow and heavy, more like a large field ditch; the flat surroundings quickly flood in times of heavy rain.

This is the pastoral look of southern England, pretty villages with a brook and water meadows all around. Good for grazing grass and summer hay. Cricklade's North Meadow, now a National Nature Reserve, is one of the finest uncultivated ancient flood meadows in Britain, famous for the population of rare snake's head fritillaries which flower in April (see page 81). Historically winter flooding here, and all along the river, was not a dreaded phenomenon but an expected part of the agricultural cycle and of the rural economy. As riverside villages grew organically, local knowledge guided house building so that flood water wouldn't be too big an issue. Modern planners with their quotas and their regulations for building levels (which developers seem to ignore anyway) don't tap into the old knowledge. And yet flooding can be a scary circumstance to face up to. Anyone who lives beside a pretty brook that can turn after a few hours of rain into a swollen torrent knows of the stressful dedication to the weather forecasts, sleepless nights with rain on the windows and dread anticipation of the tap on the door with a neighbour saying "We're going under!" There is more water and it is coming faster and we don't all live like sons of the soil; is it hard luck for thinking that a cow shed might make a good design studio? Purpose-built at a level whereby most winters its owner would be happy to see it getting a good sluice out from a rising brook can mean disaster for a more modern usage.

Flooding seems to fit into three categories, more or less easy to bear. Firstly, and the least upsetting, is a flash flood caused by an overflowing brook or blocked culverts, or a combination; water comes over the threshold, wets the floors and then as soon as the rain stops, it's gone. A nasty clear-up, making sure the mud is removed before it sets to a hard brown glue, and perhaps remedial action for next time, and a line is drawn. Worse than that is to be in a river town knowing that upstream there has been exceptional weather and that the water is coming your way. Maybe it is two days away. Maybe the flood forecasters have it wrong and it will spread and diminish, but for two anxious days you are expecting the worst. Not the *very* worst necessarily, for that is reserved for the kind of floods that sometimes, with no precedent, hit towns or suburbs whose streets are built on ground describing a saucer shape: if deep water gets in, it can't get out and, the worst scenario of all, the drains back up so that floodwater is mixed with sewage. All these cause varying degrees of misery or danger (though we should be grateful that it is never on a Bangladesh scale where flooding seems to be endemic). Sandbags piled against the doorways are the telltale sign of an afflicted part of town. Do they do any good? They certainly make a householder think they are doing what they can. Their real benefit is directing and channelling water in its ceaseless quest to find lower ground, but they are never going to make a good barrier against standing water.

In January 2007 the bright sparkling waters of the Churn met the turgid Thames, swollen and muddy, to flood the water meadows around Cricklade, a not-unusual winter occurrence; this time parts of the town were under threat and local opinion was that in living memory there had never been so much water. At Cerney Wick the Thames & Severn Canal, which runs close to the river, is one of many restoration projects in the big revival of the inland waterway network; mocking the renovation timetable and with no respect for schedules, the lock involuntarily filled with water, so for the first time in decades the Thames & Severn had the appearance of a working canal.

Above: Brunel's rail bridge, Windsor;
Right: Police launch, Westminster; Below: Tower Bridge,
1983; Facing page, left: Houses of Parliament,
Westminster; Right: Kayak racing, Cookham.

Note: Map placenames in blue indicate river locks.

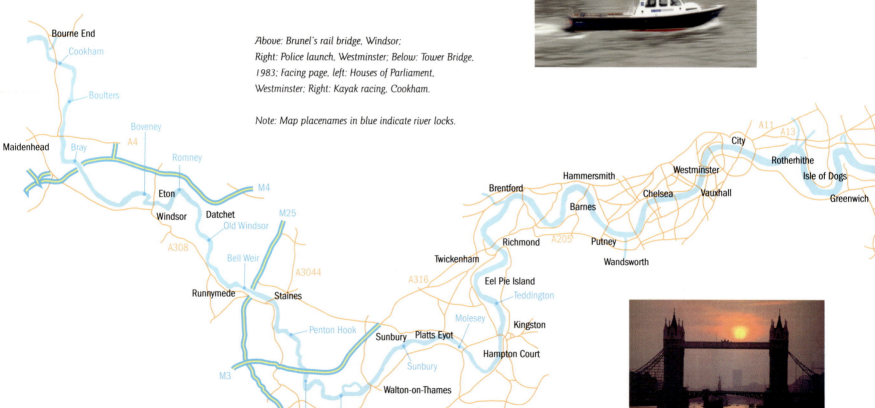

Voyaging Downstream

The Bounty

Back at Bourne End there are a couple of things to notice before heading downstream. Historically a ferry ran from the wharf at Townsend Brothers yard to serve the small community across the river where there is no road access (typical pre-war pre-planning era riverside bungalows) and the summer children who wanted to swim at the little beach. As well as the houses there is a pub, in recent times called The Bounty, and run by a man with a hook for a hand. The present owner, entertained by the idea of a pub you could only reach by ferry, took his friends and liked it so much bought it; today he runs it with the help of his wife and one of the original visiting friends, Bob Wheeler.

Although the ferry has closed, and access is now by a footpath added onto the railway bridge just downstream, there is an occasional boat to be seen at the wharf – the beer ferry supplying The Bounty. By arrangement I visit on a delivery day and find Bob rowing over a load of empty casks, to meet a lorry from the Marlow brewery with a new supply of Rebellion beer.

Above: Rebellion beer cask;
Left: Bob Wheeler ferrying the empties across the river.

Upper Thames Sailing Club

Bourne End might sound a bit aggressive, with Rebellion beer in the pub and a mascot named 'Vengeance' in the yacht club (a replica figurehead from an eighteenth-century battleship). In fact, the Upper Thames Sailing Club is a thoroughly respectable and important body, hosting open meetings including, in Bourne End week, a championship for the classic 'A Rater' single-handed yachts. On the rather grey and blustery day of my visit, the race is for the 'OK' class.

Myriad yachts are milling around waiting for the start and I am intrigued by the system of flags flying: the red and yellow one denotes the OK class, the 'Blue Peter' is raised at minus five and dropped with one minute to go. The start is signalled by the class flag being lowered; any yacht not behind the start line has to circle back to cross it.

Above: Flags at the start of the 'OK' class race;
Left: The club's mascot, 'Vengeance'.

The competitors are completing their first lap, up then back down the river, and turning at a buoy. I feel like a voyeur, for right in front of me a mini-drama is playing out. Four boats turn, and are bunched up together heading across the river, and another, caught in a squall, is coming at high speed and passing the buoy on the wrong side. It collides with the last of the four, literally knocking it over. The young, but no doubt experienced, sailor, a lad named Tom, vanishes under his sail, under his boat and in a flash he has come out on the far side and manages to right it. I am really impressed, but Tom isn't. Very quickly it is clear that there is a large gash in his hull and he has to retire. The other boat is damaged too and its skipper glumly waits his turn for the rescue boat.

There appears to be no bad feeling and as Tom walks to the club house he doesn't even glance at Vengeance.

Top: Collision on the water;
Above: Inspecting the damaged hull.

Cookham

Leaving Bourne End again the first village downstream is Cookham. This was home to Stanley Spencer, visionary and painter, who worked and lived there in the early twentieth century. Spencer used aspects of the village and the river in his paintings, but his real agenda was driven by his quest for spiritual meaning. Although the mate embraced local talent and took vicarious pleasure from his fame, she may really have approved of his religious devotion which she would have liked us all to share.

We did frequently go to a church on Sundays even on our river travels, particularly when we were at Clifton Hampden, but it wasn't an imperative. Not so for our visiting Catholic cousin, who wrote this diary entry in July 1948 offering a more rigourous take on life, duty and retribution: '*10pm, people camping on the bank made a terrible noise till 11 saying things like 'shut up'. In the morning I had to go to church in Marlow so we had to start up the boat at 6 o'clock so we paid the campers back.*'

Cookham has a very pretty iron bridge which features in Spencer's work, famously combining with one of the river's annual pageants in the painting 'Swan Upping at Cookham Bridge', a print of which is in the foreground skiff. The original painting is in Tate Britain, but much of Spencer's legacy is on view in the village gallery.

Top: The Old Swan Uppers pub sign;
Above: The Stanley Spencer Gallery, Cookham;
Right: Skerne Ironworks casting;
Facing page: Cookham bridge, with Spencer's 'Swan Upping at Cookham Bridge' on view in the foreground skiff.

90

Swan Upping

Swan Upping is a ceremonial pageant, nominally to mark the birds to define ownership. The popular conception that the Queen owns all the swans is a myth: traditionally some belong to the two ancient City companies, the Dyers and the Vintners. The 'Upping' begins at Staines and progresses up river to Abingdon, a five-day voyage for the flotilla of skiffs and support boats.

Only breeding pairs of swans with cygnets are of interest: they are cornered and caught, historically in order that their beaks can be inspected (a nick on the left or right side denoted which company the bird belonged to, and no mark indicated it to be the Queen's), though today their legs are ringed for identification. It is possible that more birds are missed than noticed (up backwaters, tributaries, etc.) but, if unmarked, they are deemed to be royal. Like so many traditions with ancient beginnings, the pageantry dates from Victorian times.

Above: Swan and cygnets; Right: Men with white feathers in their hats, left to right, Martin Spencer (Vintners' Bargemaster), David Barber (Swan Marker to HM The Queen) and David Reed (Dyers' Bargemaster). Facing page, top: Skiffs encircle the swans; Below: The Queen's skiff.

I was allocated a seat in the Swan Upping flotilla from Cookham to Marlow but was a bit unlucky: the two spots where swans were expected to be had been abandoned due to the recent high river levels. So I had a pleasant drive up the river (in the Henley umpire boat *Argonaut*) following the boats of the Royal contingent and the two city companies, but relied for my picture of the skiffs encircling the swans on the Buckingham Palace press office. And in case you are feeling sorry for all the honoury rowers making that long trek: don't worry – most of the way they get a tow from the accompanying fleet of cruisers.

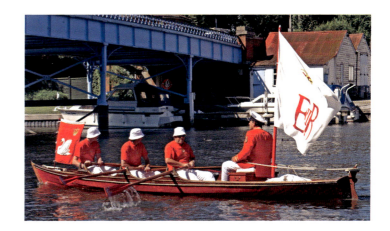

Top: Sally and Owen Peake, Longridge, at the start of Day Three of the race; Above: Dauntsey's crew, Jon Gosling and Alex McNaughton.

Canoeing – Devizes to Westminster Race

Various craft are associated with the Thames – slipper stern launches built by Andrews at Maidenhead, Salter's Steamers from Oxford, traditional flat-bottomed wherries and ferries as well as the humble punt and skiff, both of which have canvas-covered variants for camping trips. A list of local specialities would not include canoes. Yet every Easter the river is alive with hundreds of competitors paddling, mainly kayaks, in the annual Devizes to Westminster race. From tiny beginnings the 'DW' now has many classes of entry with elite racers going non-stop (taking from 15 hours upwards) while juniors in pairs take it in stages with three overnight stops on the way.

Devizes is on the Kennet and Avon Canal, cut in 1810 to provide a link to the Thames at Reading to the Avon at Bath. Initially following the Kennet valley it takes the line of the old Bath road, at times running alongside; driving down to visit my elder brother at boarding school, Dauntsey's near Devizes, it was the first canal I ever noticed. As one of the earliest to become a renovation project there were still 'dry' sections when the canoe race was first instigated, which meant a lot of 'portage' along the towpath. Then I was a schoolboy too, and although I never paddled a canoe my memory is that some from the school did, but with no official involvement.

I decided to see what vicarious pleasure I might gain by following Dauntsey's involvement in the 2008 race. Things are certainly very different today as the school had ten teams in the junior race. I went to visit them at Marlow for the start of day three: despite the blizzards that early Easter, not only were most of the crews still in the race but the school's commitment was emphasised by the presence of the headmaster, Stewart Roberts, leading the support. Sally Peake, the race starter, and her son Owen, the chief umpire, were another Dauntsey's connection – the school crews have been coached by the Peake family for twenty years.

As I arrived at the campsite at Longridge Canoe Club, the huddle of tiny two-man tents reminded me of overnight experiences of my own – in my case Mountain Marathons. Of course, the difference is that the canoeists all have their back-up teams carrying their kit and the site has toilet blocks and a café, where the MMs carry everything they need on their backs for two days and camp in a mountain wilderness. Nevertheless, the canoeists have three nights of it, and it is a severe test of personality to head out onto the wide river in a flimsy kayak in the teeth of winter weather – especially knowing that the

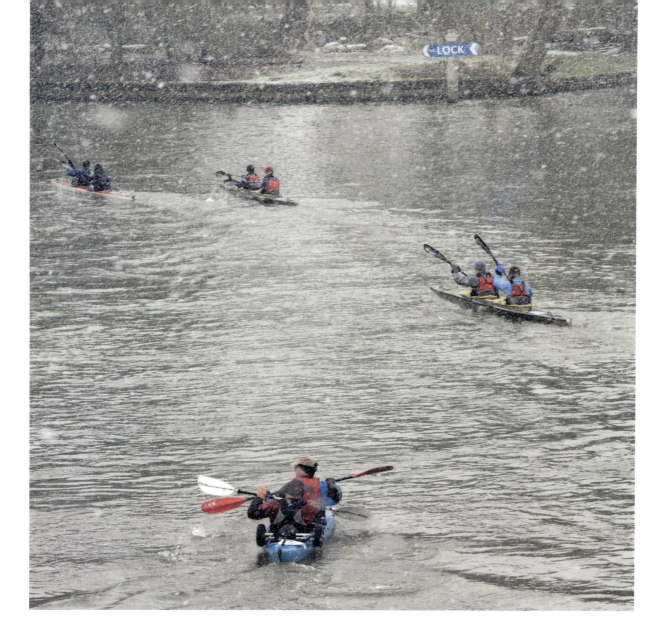

Above: Canoeing into a blizzard, Cookham.

fourth day start at Teddington would be at three o'clock in the morning (to suit the tide). Stewart Roberts told me that the school originally supported the race as an opportunity for pupils who wouldn't get into a sports team to realise achievement through endeavour. Like all things competitive it inevitably got adopted by the sporty set too. That doesn't alter the general spirit of the race, a marathon with an emphasis on teamwork and loyalty as much as commitment and stamina; taking part is a difficult challenge, to finish is a bonus and success cannot be measured just by a stopwatch.

Brunel on the Thames

Isambard Kingdom Brunel, Britain's best-loved engineer, chose the Thames as a level route away from London for his Bristol railway. At Maidenhead, Brunel was faced with a design problem, caused by the Thames Commissioners' stipulations on width and height of passage; its solution provided one of his greatest triumphs. Although the chosen crossing point could make use of an island for a central pier, Brunel was unwilling to lift the railway line, running low and level in the valley, as much as the width of such a wide arch would conventionally require. His answer was to ignore precedent and (amongst much doubt and derision) design his two brick arches with a profile so low that no flatter has ever been made.

The results of Brunel's extravagant, one might say say flamboyant, inventiveness were more than mere technical achievement. His railway could be seen as a metaphor for the extraordinary pace of change that the industrial revolution had imposed on the social fabric of the country. That is exactly the way the renowned artist J.M.W. Turner saw it. His painting 'Rain, Steam and Speed' shows one of the Great Western 'flyers' crossing over the Thames at Maidenhead, a scary fiery spectre blurring into the night sky as it sweeps at previously unimagined speed over the impossibly flat arched bridge, a representation of progress rushing into the unknown.

There are less remarkable brick bridges, over the Kennet where it joins the Thames at Reading, and twice across the Thames itself above Goring, where the railway, squeezed into the river valley under the scarp edge of the Chiltern Hills, crosses at Gatehampton and finally re-crosses at Stoke to head for the White Horse Vale (see page 47). In 1950 we boys didn't know who Brunel was but, with *Sir Humphrey* moored close to the viaduct, train spotting seemed to rival fishing; this was a reflection of home life, for as well as watching the great Kings and Castles of the Great Western pausing for breath in Wycombe station yard (see page 69), we spent patient hours on Saunderton Bank waiting for the infrequent trains on the Birmingham line. Then, aged ten and twelve, we graduated to travel anywhere within day trip range; a favourite was Reading General where the unusual three-track layout between the main platforms meant that non-stopping Penzance trains seemed to charge straight at us before before hurtling past in a screaming blur. We didn't realise it but these were the last days of steam: moored up at Shiplake in 1950 the diary notes: *'rail trip to Henley by diesel, back by ordinary train'* – 'ordinary' meaning steam!

Above: The Cambrian Coast Express on Saunderton Bank, 1953.

Just downstream from Maidenhead is an equally splendid though totally different bridge – that carrying the Windsor branch railway line over the river. Built in 1849 of riveted wrought iron, this triple 'bow and string' girder looks so modern that the day I first saw it, working on my Brunel book, I cursed the fact no one had told me there was a twentieth-century replacement. When I realised I was wrong, I was amazed that this wonderful example of simple functionality, so ahead of its time, is not more noticed.

On my second visit to Windsor I found a couple of lads sunning themselves on the bank by the bridge. I asked if they also swam there. "Well, we're jumpers," one said. Without more ado, or me knowing what he meant, he vanished under the arch and a moment later appeared high on the front 'bow' girder waving and, walking to the top, jumped. He swam ashore and back up on the bank was quite dismissive of his feat – he might as well just have sauntered off to buy an ice-cream. Naively I asked him his name. "Just call me Tricky," he said, and went back to sunbathing.

 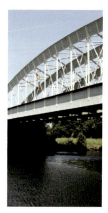 

Top: Maidenhead Bridge;
Above: 'Tricky' jumping from Windsor rail bridge.

Windsor and the musical revolution.

I remember *Sir Humphrey* taking us down river past Windsor Castle and Windsor Great Park; as boys we visited the state apartments more than once. More interesting than the Victorian flim-flam is the sheer physical presence of the castle on Windsor's unlikely rocky bluff and its long history of dominance of the river, bracketed only with the Tower of London as an important defensive site.

With *Sir Humphrey* fading into history, more vivid are the recollections of Windsor as a music venue. When Buddy Holly died in 1959 and Chuck Berry went to prison, for some of us the music died too. Emerging from the dire sounds of the very early sixties, the Beatles woke me out of a teenage hibernation: but never mind Liverpool, we had our own local Mecca in Windsor – the Ricky Tick club, a first-floor room at the Star and Garter pub by the town station. In the spring of 1963 the Rolling Stones were playing their first dates further down the river at Richmond's Crawdaddy Club and, famously, at the Eel Pie Island hotel; with their reputation spreading (and parental outrage simmering), our friday nights were as likely to feature them as Long John Baldry, Cyril Davies or Alexis Korner. The tiny room was packed so tight that the floorboards bounced, and dancing meant 'pogo'; girls sat on shoulders and sometimes reared into the sultry swinging roof fan which could do little to clear the heady atmosphere which left the most active literally soaking. On one occasion my mother caught us arriving home she was horrified by my soggy state; knowing we had been to Windsor she assumed I'd been thrown in the river!

By the summer Ricky Tick had moved just upriver to a mansion at Clewer Mead where there was more space, ventilation and ceiling height. Within months the Rolling Stones, now with a record out and a national reputation, were appearing in my wider definition of the Thames Valley. As a student photographer I caught them backstage in Wycombe Town Hall in August that year.

Top left: Machinery, Eel Pie boatyard;
Left: The Rolling Stones at High Wycombe, 1963.

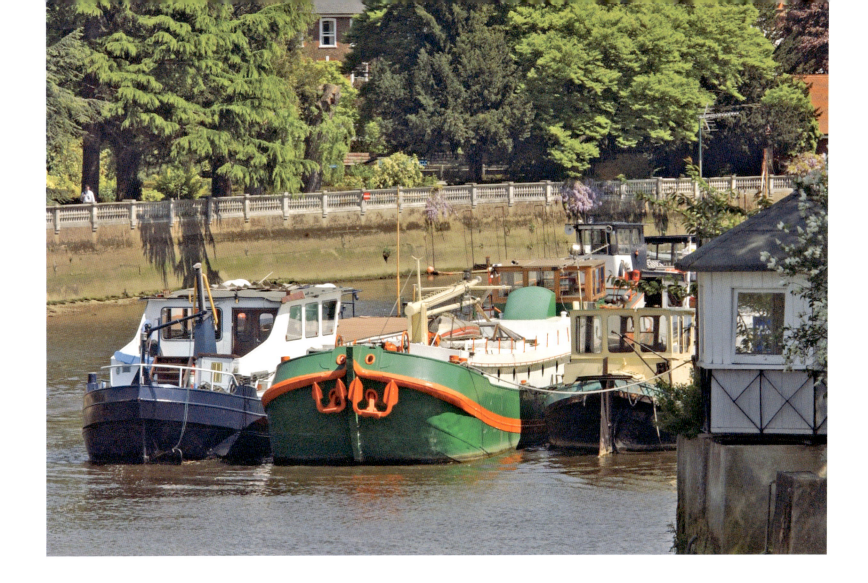

Above: Three restored barges.
Eel Pie Island.

Eel Pie Island at Twickenham has always been in my peripheral vision and, leapfrogging downstream, I am making my first visit. The music seems to have died again – I know that the hotel burned down, but I still hoped to find a remnant to hang my 1963 nostalgia on to. I have no such luck as the hotel site, occupied by a large house, is well fenced and signed with 'Private' notices. This seems out of character, for the Island still has something special – an easy-going aura of a faded hippy past. The prevalent architecture of riverside bungalows is agreeably subservient to the old sheds of the boatyard and the continuing tradition of space being available for renovation projects is confirmed by three restored barges moored in the river. Sadly there is no parallel memorial to Keith, Mick or Brian.

Windsor – royal residence

Back to Windsor where a more traditional set of views can be had from the Eton towpath. The tiny riverside church at Boveney is under restoration and covered in scaffolding – good news for the church but not for the photographer. Dating from the twelfth century it is on the site of a wharf and was built for the convenience of bargemen. Approaching Eton itself, the castle rears up above the bridge and town, presenting a contrast in residential style with a narrowboat moored in the foreground.

I have high hopes for the two bridges named Albert and Victoria, crossing and re-crossing to Datchet, part of a redesigned road system of 1851 to avoid Home Park; sadly, I discover they were demolished in the first half of the twentieth century, though the ugly concrete replacements still bear the same names. The originals are said to have been designed by Prince Albert himself and my hope is that I'll find they were in fact a proxy Brunel design (for the Prince was a close acquaintance of the great engineer). This seems unlikely when I find an old postcard which shows Albert's single cast-iron span with outer ribs including a quantity of florid ornamentation, quite against the trend to simplicity which characterised the use of the new material. If Brunel was consulted, it is unlikely this would have been his plan – in fact, a couple of years later, while building a bridge for Albert over the Dee to Balmoral, he incurred the displeasure of Queen Victoria precisely because it had no ornamentation at all.

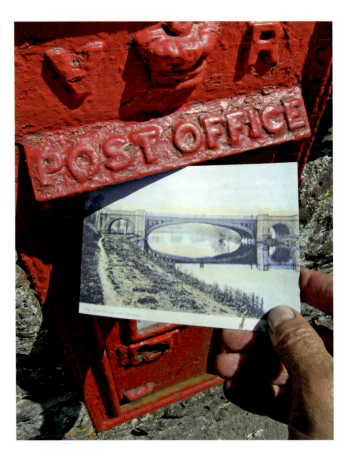

Top left: Boveney church undergoing restoration;
Left: Victorian postcard of Albert Bridge, Datchet;
Facing page: Windsor Castle from the river.

Right: Magna Carta Island;
Below: Road sign; Bottom: Bridged ditch
defines the island's boundary. Facing page, top:
Water buses frame Nuneham on the far bank;
Below: Geoffrey French at the Runnymede
boathouse.

Runnymede

There can be no better example of how the Thames intertwines with English history than the story of the Magna Carta. Between Windsor and Staines the river passes, on the south side, a wide flood meadow, Runnymede; it was at this spot that King John had a confrontation with the barons in 1215 and was forced to sign away some of his power. Magna Carta, the big plan, was a document drawn up to limit the sovereign's rights (which had been both 'divine' and absolute). Although the barons were thinking of their own interests and life did not change to any extent for the feudal masses, the long-standing concept of 'habeus corpus' was instituted – no imprisonment without a charge – which was to apply to all men, free or indentured. Over the centuries this became a basic tenet for all modern democracies (although it is this very feature that Britain, of all countries, seems intent on eroding at present).

The meeting, and signing, is supposed to have taken place on what is now known as Magna Carta Island. While this may have been chosen for security reasons, it might also have been to satisfy a simple practical need. In wet weather Runnymede was a marsh, and the higher ground of the island may have been the driest spot to sit about on. This possibility is borne out by the old road sign, and by anecdotal evidence that the river road wasn't built until 1947 (presumably late in that year, when the infamous floods had subsided).

From Runnymede the boundaries of the island itself are very difficult to differentiate from the line of the far bank, being separated by the smallest of ditches. The prominent white house is said to incorporate the ruins of a twelfth-century nunnery, itself built there to commemorate the signing of Magna Carta.

Public access to Runnymede is thanks to Lady Fairhaven who gave the meadows to the National Trust in 1931. For many people this is merely a fine riverside picnic area, with a funfair and cafés; those with a sense of history can take boat trips past the island from the French Brothers boathouse. Although this business has the look of so many Thames boatbuilders that have passed down through the generations, in fact Geoffrey French and his two brothers bought the boathouse (which had been the summer house for a big estate – presumably Lady Fairhaven's) 'only' thirty years earlier. Still they have their own sense of history: the pride of their fleet is the ex-Salter's *Nuneham*, dating from 1890 and restored to steam.

Staines

Part of Lady Fairhaven's bounty at Runnymede was to commission Lutyens to build gatehouses at the approach from Windsor and at the far end of the meadows towards Staines.

Staines was the upper limit of the City of London's authority over the Thames and the London Stone (said to be a replica) marked this point. There are similar stones at Canvey Island and Isle of Grain.

Above: London Stone, Staines;
Left: Lutyens gatehouses at Runnymede.

Shepperton

I drive to Shepperton as I know there is still a working ferry crossing to the Chertsey bank; though the ferry boat is not traditional or a thing of beauty it still performs a continuing useful role and as such should be celebrated. A notice by the brass bell says 'Ring for the ferry only on the quarter hour', which I did, but maybe it was lunchtime. Then another less than usual sight took my attention, a tug coming down through the lock with a couple of working barges heading for the Environment Agency depot in Sunbury.

Ticking time meant I never saw the ferry in action – on my way through Lower Sunbury I had caught a glance of what looked very like *Sir Humphrey* and I needed to investigate that (see page 12).

A few days later I travel up the Chertsey side of the river looking for the Wey Navigation. *Sir Humphrey* had gone through Shepperton and up the Wey to Addlestone on one of its rare downriver trips to visit friends. Perhaps the Wey is easier to find in a boat: I find myself confused and frustrated by all the double yellow lines and have to content myself with the kayakers practising white water in the weir.

Above: Bell for Chertsey ferry;
Below: Environment Agency tugs.
Facing page: Kayaks in
Shepperton Weir.

Teddington

On the way downstream I pass Platts Eyot again. Heavily industrialised by Vickers in the war, the ferry across to the island proved inadequate for the reputed three thousand workers, and a rather utilitarian footbridge was erected. Today Platts is home to a distinctly shabby assortment of commercial units, with boats to match moored along its river edges.

Teddington is the point at which the Thames is said to go tidal. This is and isn't true. Only exceptional tides reach above, but there is not much rise and fall below either; this is because there is a so-called 'half-lock' downstream from Richmond Bridge which only operates at low water. And is that a mistake, putting Teddington 'locks' in the plural? No; as well as a set of rollers for canoe or punt portage, there are three parallel 'pounds' – a small lock for rowing boats (known as the 'coffin'), a medium one for launches and a huge, almost two-hundred-metre giant which was designed to take a tug and six barges.

Above: Bridge to Platts Eyot;
Left: Teddington Weir footbridge;
Facing page: Teddington Weir.

Above: Rowing boats at Richmond Bridge; Below right: Thames Hare and Hounds training at Petersham; Facing page: View from Richmond Hill.

Richmond

Downstream past Petersham the vast acres of Richmond Park can be glimpsed on the hill to the east. In reverse, from the hill itself there is the classic view of the river winding away upstream through the verdant landscapes of Marble Hill and Petersham Meadows. There is an even more bucolic moment downstream as the river is sandwiched between the gardens of Syon House and Kew, but unfortunately no viewpoint to do it justice.

Thames Hare and Hounds are the oldest cross-country running club in the world, an offshoot of Thames Rowing Club (see page 114) whose base is in Putney. Running was the rowers' training regime, and following papertrails across Richmond Park made the hard work more fun. I ran with Thames for two or three years in the mid-seventies – Wednesday evening training sessions that could last from eight to twelve miles and frequently included a section of towpath at Petersham. During that time the club's century-old headquarters, a room over an outbuilding at The Kin'gs Head in Roehampton (whose facilities were a primitive gas-fired boiler and a dozen hip baths) burned down in a fire; relocating to an attic over the changing rooms by the Robin Hood roundabout playing fields made almost no difference to our training runs, though sadly modern showers consigned the old zinc baths to history, and the idiosyncratic geyser was replaced with a set of electric switches. Three decades on, could consistently better results be credited to better bathing?

London's river

It is convenient now to refer to the Thames as 'London's River'. I am unsure of the implied subservience; perhaps we could call London the 'City of the Thames' ?

The first tangible sign that the pastoral tranquillity of the upper river is finally past is the sight of Brentford's tower blocks. On the south bank, completely screened from the river, lie the arboreal wonders of Kew Gardens; opposite is the junction of the Thames and the Grand Union Canal. Below 'Thames Lock', a boatyard with an industrial flavour gives a nostalgic foretaste of the old working river ahead.

Housing and industry alternate on the river banks now; below Chiswick Bridge, standing forlornly next to its abandoned jetty, the old Mortlake Brewery is probably best known as featuring in University Boat Race commentaries, like the Harrods Depository downstream. We may be on the that famous Putney to Chiswick race course, but for me the towpath on the section between Barnes railway bridge (which carries a footpath) and Hammersmith Bridge is remembered as part of my five-mile training run when I lived in Chiswick – a two-mile leafy breather from the city streets.

The railway crossing at Barnes is in fact two bridges. The earliest, built in 1849 by Joseph Locke, colleague of the Stephensons and friend of Brunel, has three cast-iron spans; now abandoned, it still stands next to the bow and string girders of its 1895 replacement by Edward Andrews, giving the appearance of a single composite structure.

Left: Barnes railway bridge;
Right: Hammersmith Bridge;
Far right: Jetty, Mortlake Brewery
and Chiswick Bridge.

Barnes to Wandsworth

The big bend of the river below Hammersmith Bridge would historically have been flood meadows; in the late nineteenth century the Metropolitan Water Board utilised the area as reservoirs. In 2002 there was a kind of reversion with the opening up of a hundred acres of the site as the Barnes Wetland Centre. This is home to various non-native species as well as being a drop-in destination for natives such as herons (as well as the inevitable London pigeons). The centre is busy with primary school visits as well as serious birdwatchers.

The river road upstream of Putney bridge, the Embankment, simply drops into the water like a continuous launching ramp; for long stretches the land side is lined with the boathouses of rowing clubs, including Thames, whose Victorian predecessors started the Hare and Hounds training on Wimbledon Common.

As the big oxbow of Barnes finally turns east, the River Wandle joins from the south London suburbs. Until 2006 this was the site of Young's Brewery who famously stuck with horse-drawn drays. The claim was that, unlike a big City brewery, this was not for showy publicity but was simply the most economic method of local delivery. When I photographed there in 1970, there were stables and blacksmiths as well as barrel-makers and wheelwrights. Today it has all gone and Wandsworth and Battersea are best known for their new blocks of riverside apartments.

Above: View from The Embankment to Putney Bridge.
Facing page, top left: Australian Black Swan, Barnes Wetland Centre;
Far left: Dray drawn by shire horses, Young's Brewery, 1970;
Left: Thames Rowing Club boathouse.

Top: St Paul's Cathedral from Bankside; Above: Damien Hirst- decorated 'Clipper' boat; Right: McDonald's sign outside County Hall.

On the Tideway – with the tourists

On the south side, from Lambeth Bridge downstream, the river's wide promenade is contained by the Tudor brickwork and the low-rise stone of the Bishop's Palace, followed by the high modernity (well, it was back in the sixties) of St Thomas's Hospital. Opposite is the 'mother of parliaments' and sandwiched in between is the Thames. Not too enticing. Clusters of out-of-season 'waterbuses' pull against the ebb tide, apparently poised in a fine balance of summer need and a trip to the breaker's yard; devoid of the elegance of the upper Thames launches, or the old steamers, they are mostly what the mate would have called 'floating greenhouses' (a term she applied to cruisers with too much glazing in their oversized superstructures). Right in front of the House of Commons terraces, a small barge carries what appears to be a garden shed on its deck and a pile of spare chairs, also hoping for a good season ahead.

By the underpass at Westminster Bridge, crowds are grouping and re-grouping in front of Big Ben and streaming past to reach the big attraction of the London Eye. On the way they must run the gauntlet of the hot dog stands and snack bars; I can't help feeling a twinge of sadness at seeing London's ex-seat of government, veteran of the war of words with Mrs Thatcher opposite, diminished and derided, with its river entrance re-branded as 'McDonalds County Hall'. On the day of my visit, Londoners are at their ballot boxes and Mayor Ken Livingstone, long ousted from the building, is being voted out of office too.

Things can only improve and the big wheel is a true spectacle, and viewpoint. Further downstream are the buildings of the South Bank Arts Centre, a world-class array of theatres, cinema, galleries and concert halls. The famously brutalist concrete architecture is not everyone's cup of tea but the cafés and restaurants undeniably are an improvement on what I have passed.

Adding a touch of colour to the scene is a Damien Hirst-decorated 'Clipper' boat. Shaped like a long-nosed but wingless waterborne Concorde, it carries art-lovers, comfortably and discreetly seated behind the dark glass of its saloons, between Tate Modern at Bankside and Tate Britain at Millbank.

*Above: Houses of Parliament,
Westminster; Overleaf: View
upstream from Tower Bridge.*

Meanwhile across the river at Westminster Pier the waterbuses are again in evidence, offering trips downstream in a variety of packages to Tower Bridge, Greenwich, or even the Barrier. The boats themselves may not be handsome, but there can be no better way to see London's river and the sights, modern and historic, that line its banks.

Above: Graveyard, Cooling.
Below: Chatham and Dover Railway
emblem, Blackfriars.

Facing page: Turner's 'Moonlight on
Millbank' outside Tate Britain, Millbank;
Overleaf: The author comparing Kokoschka's
1926 painting to the view today.

On the Tideway: art and culture

Over the centuries England's greatest river has inspired and challenged artists, visionaries and men of science. In the world of art, the sheer visual excitement of light on water in combination with the particular detail and buzz of river life has inspired great names including Canaletto, Monet and Whistler.

Upstream at Cookham we have already met Spencer, and at Maidenhead noted Turner's take on Brunel's work. Turner was born in London in 1775 and ten years later went to live by the river at Brentford; he was a prolific painter of the Thames, his subjects ranging from quiet pastoral landscapes at Abingdon to high drama in the estuary. The legacy of his own huge collection, including 'Moonlight at Millwall' and many more views of the river, is in Tate Britain.

One more visitor, a favourite of mine: a century after Turner, Oscar Kokoschka visited London to paint, returning in 1938 as a refugee. As a student in 1965, I first became aware of his vibrant Thames paintings when I was working as an assistant to Snowdon, who had just published *Private View* – a wonderful photographic study of the art scene in London. (I came too late to help with the photography; my role was printing photos for the press in the palace darkroom). Kokoschka's vision was to choose the highest possible viewpoints, combining foreground detail with the long views of the river snaking away into its huge hinterland. 'Large Thames View, 1926', featuring the old Waterloo Bridge, was painted from the eighth floor of the Savoy Hotel, one of a pair looking upstream and down.

Although Charles Dickens was a writer of and about Victorian London the low-lying marsh lands of Essex and Kent feature frequently in his novels. The river runs as a thread through his work and perhaps the fog, so frequently encountered, is a metaphor for the seething difficulties of life in Victorian London. *Great Expectations*, the best known of his novels, features the graveyard at Cooling (though it isn't named) where the convict Magwitch (on the run from one of the prison hulks moored in the mud) intimidates young Pip. Along with William Hogarth's prints, Dickens provides our favourite views of Victorian London, perhaps because they make us feel so much better about modern life.

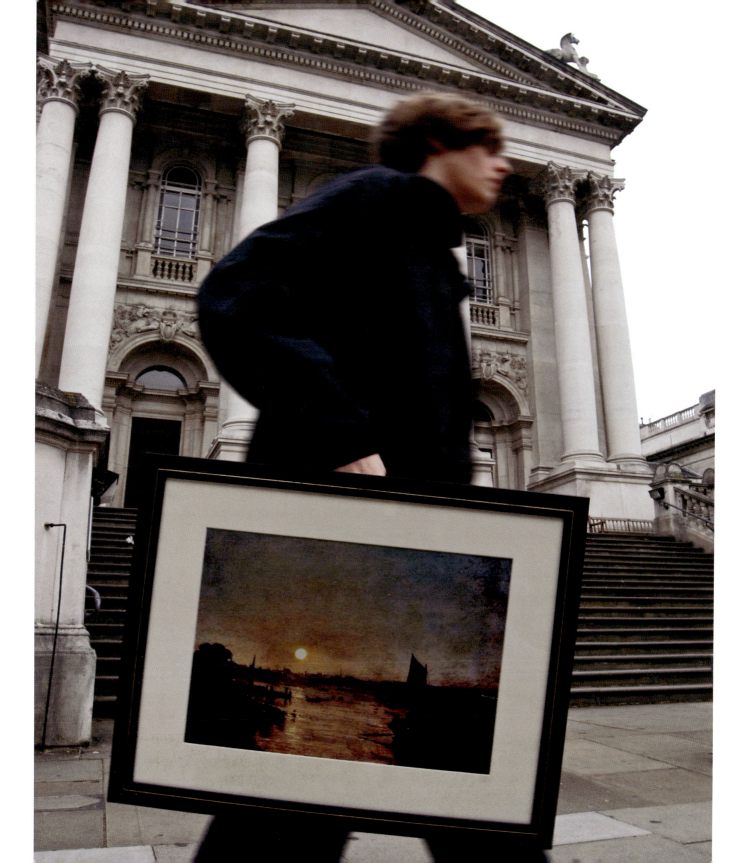

Above: Bronze figure, Vauxhall Bridge, one of eight representing the arts and sciences.

Facing page, top: Millennium Bridge from Bankside; Below: View from Westminster Bridge, looking towards Lambeth.

On the tideway: London's bridges

In the mid-nineteenth century engineers were feted as celebrities; today it is the high-profile architects who steal the limelight, while the engineers, without whom their projects would be nothing, are relegated to the wings. The Millennium Bridge, London's first new crossing for a hundred years, linking Tate Modern to Saint Paul's, was much celebrated on its opening day — until crowds started to walk across it, when it started wobbling! The early adulation was for the architect, Sir Norman Foster, but as soon as the problem became evident the blame was credited to the engineers, Ove Arup. Happily, modifications saw the bridge stabilised and reopened in 2002.

London Bridge was first built by the Romans, out of wood in AD43. How many rebuilds there were is not known, but it is documented that in 1013 a raiding party of Danes roped their warships to the bridge and, rowing downstream, pulled it down. Other sources claim that in that year the old Saxon bridge was burnt as a defensive measure. Perhaps the Danes pulled down the charred remnants? In 1209 the first stone bridge was built, financed by a wool tax. Massive piers very close together meant the bridge acted as a partial barrage, with the tide rushing through the narrow channels (passengers in the watermen's boats were said to get out and walk around what were in effect dangerous weirs). Over the centuries it became the bridge of legend, with a complete city street perched on it and a water-driven mill at each end further inhibiting flow; at the south end one span was a drawbridge where traitors' heads were displayed on spikes.

Old London Bridge was nothing if not solid and stood for 700 years. Early in the nineteenth century Thomas Telford drew up a grand design for a replacement, but the job went to another well known engineer, Sir John Rennie. In 1967 Rennie's bridge was deemed inadequate and was sold to a development company, who moved it stone by stone to Arizona (where a watercourse was built specially for it to cross!) Possibly apocryphal is the story that the Americans thought they were buying Tower Bridge, whose image so represents tourist London abroad. The modern utilitarian London Bridge is of concrete, and its most exciting aspect is the red floodlighting at night.

By 1800 there were still only three stone bridges in London, Westminster and Blackfriars having joined London Bridge in 1750 and 1769 (replaced with today's bridges in 1862 and 1869). During the nineteenth century many others sprung across the river, often at old ferry sites (for example, Lambeth Bridge is sited at the end of Horseferry Road). Others were replacements for dated wooden structures, for

instance at Fulham (which was re-named Putney) and at Battersea; these bridges were in a constant state of poor repair, with toll revenues unable to keep up with maintenance. Against all our perceptions of Victorian government, an intervention by the Metropolitan Board of Works (MBW) saw these bridges purchased in the late 1870s to be demolished; the prolific Jospeh Bazalgette (MBW chief engineer) built new ones which, when opened in 1886, were toll-free.

Upstream connections include William Tierney Clark, engineer of the very pretty Marlow suspension bridge of 1836, who preceded that with Hammersmith in 1824 (subsequently altered in 1884 by Bazalgette) and Sir Giles Gilbert Scott, whose grandfather built Clifton Hampden, designing the new Waterloo Bridge in 1942 (reputedly constructed with all-female labour).

Two more bridges

I am sorry not to mention every other London bridge, but there are two that cannot be left out. My own favourite, and arguably the prettiest of the bunch, is Albert, a suspension bridge built in 1871 to link Battersea with Chelsea. For many years when I lived in Clapham this was my umbilical with a colour processing laboratory in Old Church Street; some days I crossed over six times and despite traffic jams, closures and ridiculous 'no right turn' signs, I always loved it. Painted in pastel colours, like icing on a fantasy wedding cake, it also looks fabulous when its array of fairy lights shape up against a dusky sky.

Above: Tower Bridge;
Facing page: Albert Bridge.

Finally, Tower Bridge, iconic totem of tourist London, is unique with its centre-lifting roadway for the passage of tall ships. Its structure is deceptive: the heavy stonework, designed to blend with the ancient Tower of London close by, is really a cladding. The strength of the building is in a huge iron frame, vital to the stability of the hydraulic-driven, steam-powered mechanisms (today replaced by electricity), which had to be on a scale sufficient to lift each thousand-ton roadway section. The ubiquitous Bazalgette is linked to both these bridges: Albert was strengthened by him in 1884, but with Tower Bridge, his MBW position probably allowed him a only a nominal advisory role.

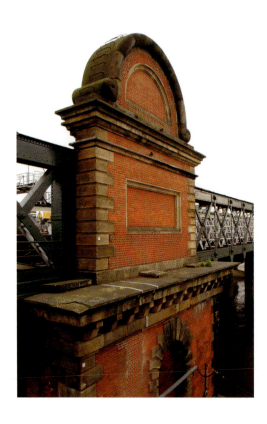

Brunel in London

Isambard Kingdom Brunel, Britain's favourite engineer, learned his trade as his father's apprentice. Marc's big project was a Thames tunnel at Rotherhithe for which he had invented a 'shield' – a huge device to protect the tunnellers until their excavations could be shored up – which was instrumental in securing an Act of Parliament to go ahead in 1825.

At the age of twenty (with his father unwell) Brunel took on the job of engineer in charge. Two years later, a shingly section of the river broke into the workings: Brunel's response was to climb down a rope into the flood and rescue a drowning worker. When another flood killed six men, Brunel, caught at the work face, was lucky enough to be washed unconscious to the surface in the shaft. The tunnel project was put on hold for a decade (and was later completed by Marc); Isambard Kingdom was sent away from London to recuperate. The Brunel's twin tunnels are in use today as part of the East London underground line and the building over the Rotherhithe shaft houses the Brunel London museum.

Another interesting Thames location connected with Brunel is at Charing Cross, where he built a suspension footbridge, soon replaced by the present Hungerford Bridge. An early Fox Talbot photograph shows that the red brick abutments, still in use by the current railway bridge (and easily visible from the modern footbridges), were the bases of the suspension towers built by Brunel. Nearby, on the embankment, stands a fine statue of the great engineer.

Further east, it's worth noting a site that isn't a river crossing but the yard where Brunel's third and last steam ship was built. Far too big for Bristol Docks, the SS *Great Eastern* was Brunel's final grand statement, built for him by John Scott-Russell (with much acrimony, as they were both prima donnas) at Millwall on the Isle of Dogs. *Great Eastern* was longer than the river was wide, so the launch (which was supposed to be a free slide but took months of pushing with hydraulic jacks) had to be sideways.

Just inland from the subsequently built Millwall embankment, the huge baulks of timber on which the *Great Eastern* was built and which served for the troublesome launch, have recently been excavated and remain as a memorial. The photograph taken at this spot by Robert Howlett, of Brunel with top hat, cigar and launch chains in the background, is perhaps as famous as the subject himself. This most wonderful portrait makes such a powerful statement that I believe it underpins the fame and hazy glorification of the maverick engineer.

Above: Portrait of Brunel on launch timbers of SS Great Eastern, Millwall.
Facing page, top: Hungerford Bridge, abutments;
Below: Brunel plaque, Rotherhithe.

Top: Bust of Joseph Bazalgette,
Charing Cross; Above: The Embankment
by Waterloo Bridge; Facing page:
Crossness Pumping Station.

Joseph Bazalgette

If art is defined as man's intervention with nature could I include engineers as artists too? Appropriately sited on the Embankment at Charing Cross is a bust of Joseph Bazalgette, perhaps the most important man in the shaping of London and the river. To understand the magnitude of his achievements, consider the murky, mucky state of London in the early nineteenth century. For centuries human waste, deposited in cesspits, was cleared at night for distribution as fertiliser on fields close to London. As the population rapidly rose (doubling in the first forty years of the century) this system broke down; In 1847 a government commission set up to tackle the problem made a false move – abolishing the cesspits. With sewage diverted into drains and tributaries, the Thames became London's sewer. The first noticeable effect was the smell – bad or worse depending on the weather. However, as the river was also London's water supply, its much worsened state soon caused severe outbreaks of cholera with many thousands dying in the years around 1850.

In 1856 the Metropolitan Board of Works (MBW) was formed, with Bazalgette as its chief engineer; but, although it was understood by then that cholera was a waterborne disease, nothing could be done through lack of funding. It was only in the year of 'the great stink', 1858, when Members of Parliament had to hang drapes soaked in disinfectant across their doorways, that money miraculously became available and Bazalgette was able to implement a radical scheme. Throughout London existing drains were to be connected to huge new mains sewers which would run several miles east before discharging into the river. The flow would be by gravity, but pumping stations were required at the 'outfalls'. Equally important for the future of London and the river, these new sewers, following along the north and south banks, would be buried under newly reclaimed land creating the embankments we know today. The river was narrowed but contained within hard banks which, increasing the speed of the currents, improved the scouring effects of the tidal flows. Despite the enormous benefits this scheme delivered, build-up of sewage where it was dumped was frequently washed back up the tidal river; two decades later chemical treatment was instigated and only liquid waste emptied at the outfalls. Solid residues were transferred to 'sludge boats' and taken out to sea for dumping. Of course today that is not allowed either – much is now incinerated (generating electricity) or turned into fertiliser – a modern, but hygienic, reflection of the old days of 'night soil'.

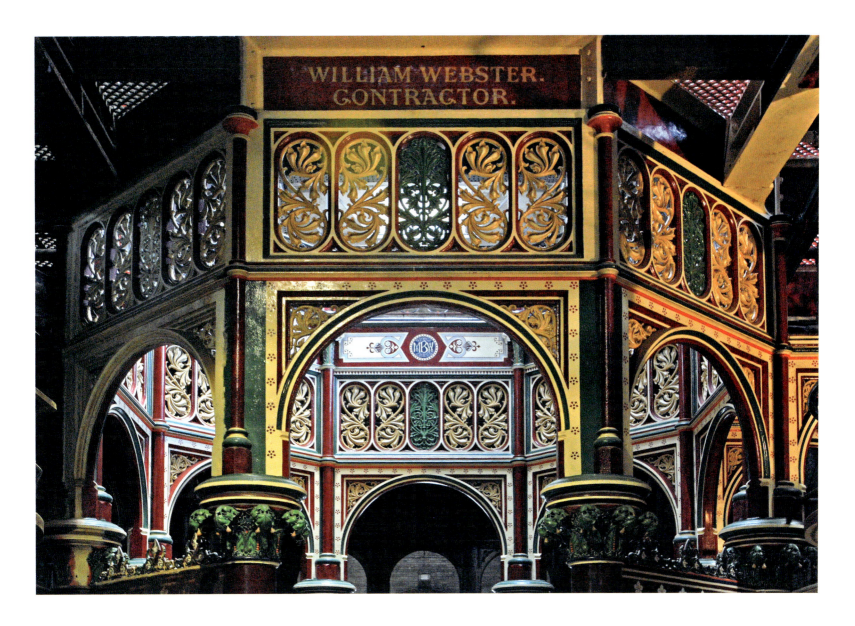

I manage to visit Crossness (Tuesdays or Sundays only by arrangement) which is on the site of a modern sewage works near Thamesmead. The building itself is Grade I listed, but it is what it contains that is really special: the original set of four rotative beam engines from 1865 is the largest in the world. Perhaps because I am not an engineer, the real spectacle is going through the doorway and meeting the most fabulous cast-iron screening, on a scale that gives a feeling of entering an industrial cathedral. As I said already, perhaps we could call Bazalgette an artist too.

131

Above: Limehouse Reach, and waterman, 1983; Facing page: Tug with containers, Waterloo.

On the Tideway: working river

As the importance of London as the country's trading hub grew, it became clear that the arrangements for seagoing ships on the Thames was inadequate. The shortage of mooring at the riverside quays and jetties, coupled with the inconvenience of ships dropping onto the mud at low tide, led to the creation of 'enclosed docks', large pools set away from the river with tidal locks at the entrance and quays lined with dedicated warehousing.

Rotherhithe, on the south side of the River, had a long association with seafaring; it was from here that the *Mayflower* set out for North America in 1620 and where, at the end of that century, Surrey Docks were constructed. A hundred years later, West India and East India Docks were built on the north side in the Isle of Dogs and Wapping. By then the size of ship was an issue for berthing at the river jetties; a secondary problem was the huge scale of pilfering along the riverside, and the new docks were built with high brick walls all around.

With the advent of containers, which could go straight from lorry to ship, the days of the old docks and their warehousing were numbered; from 1960 onwards, London's large enclosed docks went into steep decline as trade became centred downriver at the modern facilities of Tilbury. Today on London's river, white cruisers and waterbuses far outnumber the once commonplace scene of a tug towing a string of barges: such a rare sighting is most probably a cargo of waste disposal containers on their way downstream from Wandsworth. Although the enclosed docks are a thing of the past it is a misconception to think that there is no trade left on the river itself. The 2007 *Port of London Handbook* lists fifty-six working wharves – three of them above the Tower as high as Fulham, and the rest running from Rotherhithe to Canvey Island. Many of them, directly serving particular industrial facilities, deliver a diverse range of bulk cargoes – sand and aggregates, sugar and oil. Despite the eclipse of the traditional docks themselves, the PLA's claim is that London is the busiest port in the south of England.

Above: 'Blue Bridge', West India Dock, 1977.

Docks and Docklands

By 1970, developers dreamed that areas like the Isle of Dogs could become a boom housing area, the attraction being not the docks themselves but the riverside locations, and the proximity to the City of London. They were ahead of their time, for they hadn't reckoned with the attitude of the 'Islanders' who, already incensed by the threat of loss of jobs, were actively hostile to incomers. I worked for two companies who did build successful estates there. In 1977 Bovis built Capstan Square, having had the confidence to go ahead even though another developer's already completed terrace stood totally unsold with its windows boarded up. This was followed in the early eighties by Wates's Jamestown Harbour on old West India Dock.

For a decade as the docks inexorably shut down the area simply became abandoned open space, a huge kids' adventure playground. In 1982, a year after the final closure, to get some rapid action on this unused and apparently unloved and unwanted derelict land, the Docklands Enterprise zone was created. The London Docklands Development Corporation, set up by Michael Heseltine for Mrs Thatcher's government, had sweeping and unprecedented powers. For new buildings the need for planning permission would be swept aside and for businesses, rates would not initially be payable. Although the local authority did not like this high-handed deal, which cut them out completely, it did have an electrifying effect on development.

In 1985 I worked on the LDDC annual report for the following year and can attest to the pace of change, particularly around the old West India Docks. However, although extensive, the new commercial developments were usually low-rise and on a relatively modest scale. Yet already there was talk of some of this newly built enterprise having to make way for building on a much bigger scale: the huge towers of Canary Wharf were coming, redefining these areas of east London as an adjunct of the City itself.

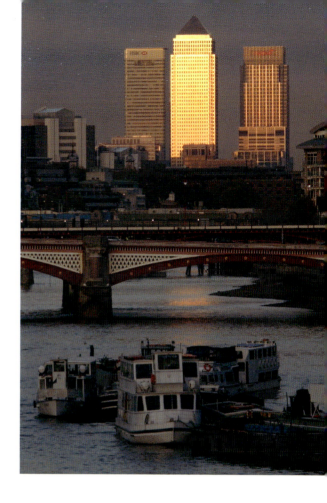

Top right: Canary Wharf; Middle: South Quays Plaza, 1985. Right: Housing and warehousing, Isle of Dogs, 1985.

Top: Family Picnic in Island Gardens, adjacent to the foot tunnel entrance, looking towards Greenwich, 1983; Above: Queen Elizabeth II Bridge, Dartford. Facing page: Thames Barrier, Woolwich Reach.

The final crossings

Apart from ferries, Tower Bridge was the lowest crossing until supplemented by the Victorian tunnels of Rotherhithe and Blackwall and the Greenwich foot tunnel. Today the modern tunnel and Queen Elizabeth II bridge at Dartford provide a link for London's M25 motorway ring. In between, the Woolwich Ferry still runs a free service connecting the old North and South Circular roads. Also free is the foot tunnel, crossing from Greenwich by the Cutty Sark to the tip of the Isle of Dogs adjacent to Island Gardens.

A unique piece of engineering amongst all these cross river routes is the Thames Barrier, sited at New Charlton a mile downstream from the O2 Arena. It is best known for the iconic look of its nine stainless steel hoods rearing up out of the water; these house machinery that can raise huge 'paddles' off the river bed to completely block any river flow – man's attempt to defy the natural forces that, it is postulated, could flood the centre of London.

If, back up at the source, you waded through the depths of my concerns over flooding, brace yourselves for a further inundation. The infant river in Gloucestershire may overflow with too much rain: the estuary can be much more scary when, infrequently, North Sea storms and a full moon combine in a 'surge'. In a narrowing estuary, a tidal surge can accelerate and increase the height of its lead wave – the effect that creates the Severn Bore.

As I stand beside the Barrier I am awed not only by the size of its famous hoods, but by the height of the 'levées' (the flood prevention banks) particularly on the downstream side. It would obviously be no use blocking the river in the face of a storm and tidal surge if it were simply to outflank the barrier; but brooding on the issue makes me wonder at the sheer scale of the potential disaster which the barrier is designed to prevent. I'm remembering a trip I made in north Mississippi to see Johnny Cash's *Big River* and how I was still a mile away when the 'levée' baulked any further progress. When Don McLean sang 'I took my Chevy to the levée but the levée was dry', he used the word to refer not to the bank itself, but to the wide space between it and the river. This was an area designed to accept flood water on a massive scale. English planners seem rarely to allow flood-prone rivers this expansive but controlled possibility, expecting to contain the water with higher and higher banks within the width of the river's low-water channel. To the east of London the Thames is flanked by wide areas of

what were, until recently, marshland: Erith, Dartford, Swanscombe to the south, Hornchurch, Rainham and Tilbury on the north side. These low-lying areas are now drained and dry behind protective banks and have been absorbed into the built environment. Rising sea levels and more frequent storms are a feature of our times; can the levées and the Barrier (too far upstream to help Erith and Woolwich) prevent the kind of disaster which overtook Canvey Island in 1953, or will we rue the development of the flood plains?

Tilbury

For several decades Tilbury has been an ever-expanding container dock, but I am visiting the separate passenger terminal to see the *Empire Windrush* plaque (see page 68). As well as the plaque, an artwork by Turner prizewinner Jeremy Deller, depicting the ship and its arrival, is on display.

Meanwhile it is a busy few minutes out on the river jetty: *Balmoral*, a classic 1950s eight-hundred-passenger coastal cruiser, is about to set off for Whitstable (where it will begin a voyage back up to Tower Bridge) and its pilot arrives on the harbour master's launch. At the same time, the small half-hourly ferry to Gravesend is ready to leave, dwarfed by a giant roll-on-roll-off lorry ferry, heading up to the modern facilities which I passed on both sides of the river by the QEII Bridge.

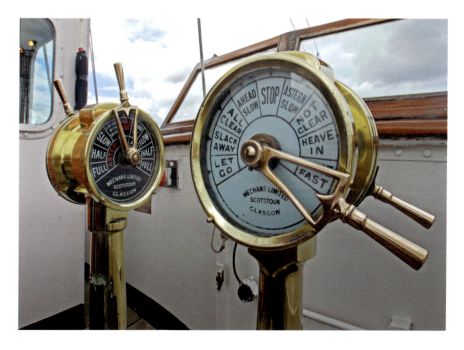

Above: Tilbury-Gravesend passenger ferry and Ro-Ro ferry; Top right: River pilot joining an incoming ship at Gravesend; Right: Bridge control gear, MV Balmoral.

Facing page: Thames estuary,
looking towards Canvey Island.
Bottom right: Isle of Grain;
Below: Swans under the flood
bank, Allhallows.

Allhallows – the end of the road

I'm driving east on the Hoo peninsular at the end of which, arguably, the Thames finally admits to being the North Sea. The grey tarmac winds like a river through a yellow landscape of widespread rape, and a broad stretch of industry-fringed water is in view to the south. My wife phones. She has just heard my message that I won't be home for the kids after school. "Why are you in Kent anyway – the Thames doesn't flow there," she claims. I have a slight wobbly, for it is true that the estuary in sight, way across flat drained meadows, is in fact the Medway. Almost immediately, I cross a rise of the promontory and to the north the Thames reveals itself, huge, with the tight-packed suburbs and oil terminals of Canvey Island glistening on the sunny Essex shore across two miles of water.

As I drop down to Allhallows the river vanishes behind its high levée; without these flood protection banks all the drained pastureland would still be tidal marshes and the settlements themselves vulnerable to storm surge. I park at the end of the road and walk to the river where, in unlikely symmetry with the stream at the source in Gloucestershire, swans are swimming on a reed-fringed pool beneath the levée. Climbing the ten-foot rise a view is revealed of far-off container ships, possibly dropping off their river pilots, quite tiny in the vast canvas of sea and sky. To the east, past grazing cattle, the refinery of the Isle of Grain marks the junction with the Medway and finally, if imperceptibly, the Thames merges with the sea.

140

Epilogue

It would have been a triumph of hope over expectation to have discovered *Sir Humphrey*, with restored mahogany and polished brass, riding proud amongst the modern cruisers in a river marina; sad to say, it must be more likely that there is a broken hulk in the mud in some forgotten creek. For the 'skipper' this seven-year adventure proved to be no flash in the pan, for when he retired he moved to the south Devon coast, joined the Island Cruising Club, bought a yacht and learned to sail. After a year or two of coastal sailing (with a reluctant 'mate'), he loaned the boat to the club and spent his time repairing dinghies, varnishing hulls and busing himself with other boaty things. The cemetery at Salcombe is high on the ridge and skipper and mate have a grand location looking out over the estuary.

Reading the diaries sixty years after my childhood travels, and revisiting the old locations, I can't help thinking that 'skipper' and *Sir Humphrey* had quite a lot in common. Knarled, weather-beaten, stoic, and, despite the best care, still liable to breakdown, they soldiered on, through regattas or through life itself, with scant regard for fashion or outside opinion. Perhaps, for me personally at least, the search which has failed to find *Sir Humphrey* has not been in vain if it has directed a spotlight onto its maverick but thoroughly worthwhile skipper and his faithful and enduring mate.

Above: The skipper with model yacht, Bourne End, 1950; Right: The mate (left, writing her diary) and the skipper's mother, Downley, 1953.

Index

Acknowledgements

Many thanks to all those who appear in this book. I am also grateful for help and advice from:

Albright Knox Art Gallery

Barnes Wetland Centre

Bourne End Marina

The Compleat Angler Hotel

Kay and Jeremy Denny

The Environment Agency

Henwood and Dean

Ann Ingleby-Lewis

Paul Manning

Andrew Morris

Roger Morris

Stephen Morris

Woody Morris

Port of London Authority

River and Rowing Museum, Henley

Brian Shaw

Tate Britain

Thurrock Museum

Mark Whitby

Photo credits

All archive and modern photos © Chris Morris, except:

32 and 33, *Herakles*, punts © Henley Royal Regatta

93, skiffs circling swans © Buckingham Palace Press Office

100, postcard © *theroyalwindsorwebsite.com*

131, photograph by the author, © Crossness Trust.

Photos of Maidenhead Bridge (page 97) and Hungerford Bridge (page 128) are reprinted from Chris Morris, *The Great Brunel* (Tanner's Yard Press, 2005). Black and white archive photos other than those by the author are by Mary Morris ('the mate').